Some books stir your soul in ways you didn't know you needed. Their stories crack you open only to piece you back together more whole than before, tucking within more hope, more light, more *why*. This is one of those books, and Liz is one of those storytellers. These pages are a haven of their own.

KAILA LUNA, writer; executive editor of *Magnolia Journal*

With ancient and original ideas, and imagery celebrating the everyday sublime, this book will leave you feeling that you have everything you need to live well—starting today. It's a beautiful and compassionate take on not just how to live, but how to *be*. Original, uncategorizable, indispensable.

SOPHIE DOW DONELSON, author of *Uncommon Kitchens* and *Style Secrets: What Every Room Needs*; former editor in chief of *House Beautiful*

A few months ago, on a difficult afternoon, I closed my laptop and brought this beautiful book outside with me. The book and I settled under a tree on a cold, sunny fall day, and Young's warmhearted writing and lovely photographs revived and inspired me. Connection, beauty, hospitality, and creativity spring up from every page, and I found myself making a list in my head of all the women with whom I want to share this special book.

SHAUNA NIEQUIST, *New York Times* bestselling author of *I Guess I Haven't Learned That Yet* and *Present Over Perfect*

As beautiful as it is touching, this book is what our overwhelmed and disconnected world needs—a reminder that we are worthy of being taken care of and that we deeply need true connection with one another. It's a call to return to the simplicity of creating warm homes and safe spaces that allow others to be vulnerable and feel supported. Liz's poetic and beautiful storytelling, paired with practical how-tos, recipes, and interactive surprises, makes *Let There Be Havens* a delightful page-turner. I highly recommend this to anyone who needs a lift to reawaken their gift of hospitality.

SARAH DUBBELDAM, founder and chief creative officer of *Darling* magazine and Darling Clothing

In *Let There Be Havens*, Liz Bell Young has probed a myriad of her own stirring life memories to write a deeply thoughtful collections of essays, each one of which stands on its own as a paean to the meaning of hospitality. I found myself relating to many of her personal stories and resonating with the emotional discovery that ties them all together—the Golden Rule of hospitality: to do unto others as you believe *they* want done unto them.

DANNY MEYER, author of *Setting the Table: The Transforming Power of Hospitality in Business*; New York City restaurateur; and founder and executive chairman of the Union Square Hospitality Group

Early on in my career, Liz taught me one of the most important truths about creating hospitable spaces: it's more impactful to make people feel seen and known than to seek perfection. People remember how you make them feel—not how much money you spend. This book is a testament to that genuine intentionality.

JENNY BUKOVEC, award-winning hospitality designer, featured in *Architectural Digest*, *Vogue*, and *Condé Nast Traveler*

I am not a natural haven maker, so on a practical level this book has given me confidence and much-appreciated tools. But what draws me back again and again stirs beneath the surface of Young's writing. Her designs are not merely designs, her daydreams not just a few stolen hours of enjoyment. She connects us with a deeper world that's easy to miss in the hustle of everyday life, a world I want to stay in—with her—as long as I can.

ANNA MITCHAEL, author of *They Will Tell You the World Is Yours*

Liz made a book into an actual haven. As soon as I opened it, I found her spirit of hospitality embodied in the pages. This book invites the reader first to be seen, known, and valued. Then it woos you to do the same for others.

CHUCK MINGO, pastor and author of *Living Undivided: Loving Courageously for Racial Healing and Justice*

How do you judge a book, if not by its cover? Even more truly, if not by its title? Deeper still, if not by its author? This work captures the longing of a mother's heart to welcome readers to their beloved place at the table. Feast on chapters infused with love, conviction, and desire. What we need more of in this world are homes filled with intention and deep, joy-filled, sacrificial love. Liz serves a timely meal between these pages. Read slow, read true. And know this: you were made for home.

ENIOLA ABIOYE, musical artist and author

Whether planning and building her dream home or accepting, at a time of great stress, a piece of chocolate from a "stranger-neighbor," Liz Bell Young shows us both how to recognize and how to create the havens, with their love and calm, we so need to sustain each of us in this challenging and frenetic world. *Let There Be Havens*, with its exquisite prose and striking photographs, is itself a haven, a place we can go to again and again for respite, guidance, and renewal.

ELLIOT RUCHOWITZ-ROBERTS, author of *White Fire: Poems*; coauthor of *Bowing to Receive the Mountain: Essays by Lin Jensen/Poems by Elliot Roberts*

Let There Be Havens is the book I've needed the last few years and didn't know it until I opened the first page. With breathtaking visuals, heartfelt wisdom, and a touch of sweetness through recipes, Liz has created a guide to crafting spaces of love and tranquility, making this book an indispensable companion for anyone seeking to create a life full of sanctuaries and connection. The book itself is a haven I will excitedly revisit many times over.

AMANDA SUDANO RAMIREZ, musical artist and songwriter, Johnnyswim

Liz writes beautifully and profoundly. But more importantly, she's right. Our world needs more havens. This book helps you envision a changed world, one haven at a time.

RUSSELL TOWNER, president of LEE Furniture Industries

It is a rare and precious gift to dream and create with an artist who has an ear so finely tuned to the whisper of the unspoken but deeply felt desires buried in our bones that she can, without a word, simply know what you need and then create a space for you to experience it. This is the magic of creating alongside Liz. With grit and poetry, Liz sees right into the soul of a place, a person, a space. Just like everything she creates, this beautiful book will awaken hearts, unveil new dreams, and empower us all to be haven makers in our own lives.

JENNIE DVORJAK CHACÓN, writer and director of *Awaited*; cofounder and pastor of Woman Camp

Whenever I read this book, my heart soaks up its gentle beauty and light, and my shoulders drop three inches. I let my breath out. And I find myself easing back into my chair, back into that sense of safety that only comes with the spirit of abundance. Liz has composed this living lullaby of a book according to the same code by which she lives: there is enough daily margin for each of us, there is more than enough to share, and as we do, our own cups of joy are doubled to overflowing.

CHARIS DIETZ, author; writing professor at Baylor University; former senior editor of *Magnolia Journal*

GUESTS

DATE	NAME	OCCASION

Use this space to keep a record of names of people you've hosted or taken care of—inside your home or somewhere along the way—whether for a shared meal, a celebration, or an overnight visit.

Let There Be Havens

let there be
HAVENS

AN INVITATION TO GENTLE HOSPITALITY

LIZ BELL YOUNG

TYNDALE
REFRESH®

Think Well. Live Well. Be Well.

Visit Tyndale online at tyndale.com.

Visit the author at lizbellyoung.com.

Tyndale and Tyndale's quill logo are registered trademarks of Tyndale House Ministries. *Tyndale Refresh* and the Tyndale Refresh logo are trademarks of Tyndale House Ministries. Tyndale Refresh is a nonfiction imprint of Tyndale House Publishers, Carol Stream, Illinois.

Let There Be Havens: An Invitation to Gentle Hospitality

Photography by Liz Bell Young, Julie Pointer Adams, Alex Davis, Madeline Mullenbach Hall, Joel Duntin, Elise Smith, Jonathan Willis, Lindsay Brown, Lydia Supinger, Craig Dockery, and Lucy Laucht. Used with permission.

Cover photograph of home provided by author and used with permission.

Author photograph by Mia Bell, © 2022. All rights reserved.

Artwork by Elizabeth Hatchett and Rebecca Weller. Used with permission.

Poetry by Eniola Abioye and Kristin Roark

Recipes by Nicole Ziza Bauer, Elise Smith, Nickey Stevenson, and Beth Thomas

Designed by Liz Bell Young, David Valentine, Jenny Bukovec, Sarah Susan Richardson, and Laura Cruise

Edited by Stephanie Rische

Published in association with the literary agency of Punchline Agency LLC.

For information about special discounts for bulk purchases, please contact Tyndale House Publishers at csresponse@tyndale.com, or call 1-855-277-9400.

Library of Congress Cataloging-in-Publication Data

A catalog record for this book is available from the Library of Congress.

ISBN 978-1-4964-8223-5

Printed in China

30	29	28	27	26	25	24
7	6	5	4	3	2	1

To my sisters

Contents

PART 3
Coming Home

PART 1 | *in the*
BEGINNING

What I Want to Be

WE WERE ALL HUNCHED AROUND A TABLE, a bunch of young art school students with riotous hearts. The room was perched at the top of a tall school building over the crowds and carts and fumes of Chicago.

Our professor had a name like Rosemary or Rosary; I can't remember anymore. But what I remember is the question she asked: "What do you want to be when you grow up?"

I knew she wasn't being rhetorical or condescending, and I must have known she wouldn't let us off the hook. She folded her wrinkled hands together, looked us all in the eyes, and waited.

Some of us looked down at our own fluttering hands, our empty laps, then finally at each other—maybe for someone to preapprove or cheer for whatever dream was roaring inside of us.

A few students seemed more eager to answer than others. Maybe they had a response on the tip of their tongues, had practiced it with parents or peers. One student said something about a cinematic masterpiece, another about the next great novel, another about Los Angeles and turning the tide. Brave things—the things we were at that tall city school to learn how to create— the things we'd pined for or promised ourselves would be worth it.

As those dreams were spoken out loud by the classmates around me, I felt my insides cracking. I knew what I was going to say because I couldn't possibly say anything else—because nothing else would have been the truth. I was the last one to speak.

"I want to be a mother." I exhaled. And dropped off the face of the earth.

The professor caught my eye as I was falling. And I stayed with her for a second, while the space in the room after I spoke didn't get filled by affirmations or further questions. I thought, *I am supposed to be here because, more than anything, I want to be an artist, make books. I am wasting everything. What is wrong with me?*

But I did want to write books. I *do* want to. I dream endlessly about sheaves of paper, collections of words and stories. I've made paper-clipped and hand-sewn books since I was a child and imagined the rest of my life as a writer, a novelist, a woman with a pen. But there, at that point in my life, I was getting knotted up and lost—in melancholy, in heaviness. The stories I was writing were tanking my heart, and I worried they would tank others' hearts too. I didn't want it anymore. I had slid in sideways and now felt stuck in a hole that was not good for others, not good for me.

I want to pick apples off trees and dream in full sun. I want to tuck children into bed. I want to help people when they're sad, tell them I understand, hand them something beautiful to wrap their hands around. I want to fix things and tidy things and put out placemats for dinner. I want to stack firewood and sweep porches and row boats. Bake a cake or two. Love an entire family both inside our home and outside of it.

I still want to write books and tell stories, but I've finally figured out why: as a way to take care.

I believe we need to mother this world back into light—to lift one another out of the darker edges and back into this gift-song of existence, one by one. Because if we aren't nourished, we wilt and fight for scraps. If we aren't held and guided and steadied, we eventually crumble. If we don't have safe spaces to release our burdens and share our brilliant dreams, we turn to things that were never meant to hold them.

We need people, places, and experiences that bring us home, feed our hopes, rock us to sleep, then wish us well in the morning as we go back into the world and find others who need what we were just given.

Some of us have never experienced havens for ourselves, but we long for them. Maybe we want our lives to be different—gentler, more at peace, more genuinely connected to others—but haven't figured out how to get there.

We can all get there.

None of us is disqualified from this effort or starting too late. None of us has fallen too far off the path to be able to step back in. You have what it takes to take care of others. You are worth being taken care of yourself.

That day in school, after I had admitted to my class what I wanted to become, the professor of roses left me a note. She scrawled it on top of one of my short stories but stapled over it, so I had to pry off the metal to see. In that tiny space, she wrote, "I want to be a mother too."

I wonder if at some point we all wander into the same place, longing to shelter and be sheltered, to love and be loved, to make havens and live inside them.

I believe so.

HAVENS ARE PEOPLE WHO SHELTER US,
PLACES THAT HOLD US,
EXPERIENCES THAT LIFT US UP.

Pick Up a Placeholder

THERE'S SOMETHING WONDERFUL ABOUT TUCKING PIECES of your life into the pages of a book—small pieces you pick up or save from your days. Maybe it's a plane ticket, a gift from a child, something you stumbled upon while taking a walk.

I think marking a book makes it even more yours—makes it a haven.

Now it becomes a shared thing, with your life and loves sticking out from the edges. And one day down the road, maybe you'll pick up this book again and rediscover these artifacts from your life, and just by touching them, you'll remember. What you wanted. What you believed. What you were moving toward.

Look around you today. Find a bookmark or two and press it into these pages. (It will also get you into the practice of picking up small, delightful things and giving them a place.)

On Your Doorstep

I USED TO MAKE HOMES IN THE WOODS behind our house when I was little. I hauled around tree stumps for chairs, set up planks of wood and old pots for pretend cooking, brought out sheets from my mom's closet for tablecloths and curtains. I loved being in those makeshift homes—those half-hidden scenes. They were places I could crawl into, let my imagination loose. And I think I also felt held there, safe.

Forts. Tents. Treehouses.

After I grew out of building tiny homes in the woods, I got a summer job working in a warehouse as an office assistant, and I tried to do the same thing there. I tried to make a haven inside a dusty office kitchen.

"We make coffee here," the manager told me, pointing at the peeling vinyl countertop and the blank walls, and I wondered if it could be something more. I wanted the men and women in hard hats and high heels to feel comfortable there in the morning, prepared for. And even if it was cheap coffee in mismatched cups, couldn't they be beautiful cups? So I took a break from filing papers one day and scrubbed the whole kitchen, got it ready. I brought in a handful of geraniums and a bowl of fruit; I swapped out the paper cups for ceramic.

I don't know if it had any effect on the employees' spirits, but it felt worth the effort. I was raised to show love for others through action, not just in theory. My sisters and I would trail my grandmother and pick up city trash, hold doors open for strangers, offer to help neighbors with their yard work. We followed my parents into homeless shelters and served meals, painted walls, held hands. We watched my parents give away big things and take care of the small things when others couldn't. And they taught us about a God who's the source of all of it, so that everything we had, had first been given to us.

I did this kind of fort building, kitchen upgrading whenever I remembered, whenever I could. I loved adding what I hoped was beauty and care into a place. But I kept doing it because it felt like what I was created to do. It synced with my heart and seemed to sync with others' hearts too. It didn't matter if it was a warehouse corner or a front-yard lemonade stand or a place to rest where the sidewalk ends. I swept and arranged and prepared. I brought in pretty scraps I picked up beside the road or at garage sales. I watched how others around me took care of people and places, and I tried to follow their lead.

Although I was on the quiet side, I started conversations when I found the courage and asked people questions and tried to take care of them that way too, even if it was only for a minute and I was young. I think I always just wanted people to feel included and watched out for. I hadn't always felt that way, so I imagine I fought extra hard to make sure others didn't have to experience the same.

So I looked for people who seemed sad and standing alone or living without. I cried when others cried. I dreamed about bringing home stray animals and offering a place for aching feet to rest. I imagined being able to give people what they were missing. I didn't know about boundaries yet or how your energy plummets if you're not also taking care of yourself. But I've been learning this along the way too.

After the wooded forts and office cleanup days, I studied social work, married Ryan, lived overseas, went back to school, got a writing degree. I was hired by a new church started for people who'd given up on church but not on God. The seats were packed, the energy was high, and artistry was prized. I hung over the shoulders of graphic designers and set builders and videographers. I learned—gradually—to create at aggressive speeds and turn ideas into real experiences and put printed words into people's hands. As a creative team, we played with all sorts of voices, tones, volumes. We experimented with natural palettes, high-definition graphics, sharp corners—then new ones with rolling hills. We paid close attention to what connected and what didn't, then we'd go back to the drawing board and dream up something new. I couldn't believe my luck.

Then I sort of found my way back to where I'd started. A few managers took vacations or had other things to do, which left me an opening to act as a creative director. I focused on designing experiences where people felt invited, offered a place at the table, given space to think or heal. I began with softness and suggestion but then recognized that soft seems more effective when it's grounded by moments of directness; it couldn't be too ethereal, or it lost its potency and ability to transform. So I tried pairing gentleness with steadiness, and imagining ways to create shelters that could also feel like freedom. This is where a new kind of hospitality became clear to me: a host can both create space and give space at the same time. It's the kind of offering that leaves room for receiving: an open door, a lamp turned on, a place prepared.

Whether or not you've ever built homes in the woods, I imagine there's something in you that wants to build meaningful moments, create something that draws people in and offers more beauty to the world—piece by piece, life by life. Maybe you'll do this with your home itself, or maybe it will be with the way you use words in stories or in conversations, the way you design events big or small, the way you lead teams or movements, the way you uniquely take care of the world around you.

What I've learned about haven making is that it can happen quick as a wink—like beaming on the person who walks into the room, putting an old plane ticket in a new book, or pulling a chair into the sunshine. But havens can also take years to build—like cultivating relationships or building a house from the ground up. This book is about both. It explores what it looks like to use and give what you have, not stretch past your means or contort your life into something that doesn't feel genuine to who you are and what you have to offer.

Right now I'm looking out my windshield marred by the fingerprints of my kids in a city parking lot full of gasoline stains and burned-out cigarettes. I'm not always in the woods hanging sheets between trees or daydreaming in the sun. But even in this daily reality—even in these stained edges of life—there is wonder. There are people to love, moments to embrace, tables to set.

I hope this book will hold wonder for you. I want it to be a place you can settle into, dip into and out of as you have the time, or something you can cart around in a bag or a bike basket, if that's the sort of way you live. Or maybe just hold it propped open at the kitchen sink and think about things you want for your life while your hands are sudsed and water pours and children or dogs or dust bunnies tumble about your feet.

I won't overpolish anything here. And this will be challenging, because I'm a romantic with a short memory. Being optimistic and seeing things in a dreamy light can be a gift, but not when you won't also look squarely through the eyes of pain and loss and the reality of a "terrible, horrible, no good, very bad day." So here, there will be both. Optimism—but also the reality of broken eggs.

I once broke a whole carton of eggs. I was fourteen and babysitting a large group of children whose parents were very particular. And right after I bumped the eggs off the refrigerator shelf and the waves of yolk and whites flooded their particular floor, the parents walked through the back door in their business suits and shocked faces and found me there in the waves. I hadn't even had a chance to get on my knees. My shame still tries to haunt me, as shame can do. I broke the eggs of someone who didn't think mistakes were okay. And it was moments like that when I felt I was too clumsy, would make too many mistakes, couldn't be in charge or finish things beautifully and well.

But in one way or another, we all break eggs on good floors, and we can't stay kneeling on the floor looking at our shame and shortfalls. We are needed in this world no matter how many times we've failed or lost sight of our worth. We are needed to take care of one another and be taken care of, and this alone makes a life worth living.

May this book be a door propped open in your direction—and may it inspire you to open the door to others. May pale morning light and dust bunnies fill you with wonder. May crumbled asphalt edges and broken eggs feel welcome to the process. May you feel held here, at home and at peace.

YOU ARE WORTH HAVENS
UPON HAVENS.

AND THE WORLD NEEDS YOU
BUILDING THEM TOO.

**HOW I WANT MY HOME
TO FEEL**

Calm and well ordered

Genuinely child friendly

*Open for people to stop by
spontaneously*

*Filled with artistic, dreamy
moments*

*Filled with engaging
conversation*

Bustling like a workshop

Marked by nourishing meals

*Like a garden, even on the
inside*

Like freedom

_____

_____

_____

_____

_____

_____

_____

_____

_____

_____

_____

_____

_____

_____

_____

_____

Beaming

YESTERDAY I PICKED UP MY NEW FRIEND ENI. When she got into my minivan, she was like a glow stick cracked open—she was beaming that bright. Her eyes were all lit up and locked into mine as if she couldn't have been happier to see me. I thought, *This is hospitality. This is giving someone an immediate haven.*

To beam on someone is to make them feel safe in your company. Fully welcomed, fully wanted. Even if that beaming can't go on forever, when it serves as a greeting or is waiting at the door, it is a powerful thing.

It's beaming on children when they first find you in the morning. Beaming on a cashier and starting a conversation instead of keeping your head down. Beaming on your spouse even if it's the twentieth time you've run into each other that day. Beaming on friends, people who look lost, people you pass on the sidewalk.

Think of the people who beam in your life. Who are they? Who makes you feel like the apple of their eye? Think about one of those people right now, and imagine them beaming on you. Sit with how that feels. Because you can deliver that same glowed-upon moment to others.

Beaming is easy and free.

It is a peace offering, an open door, a gift.

It is a reminder that every one of us matters, even if we've done nothing to deserve it.

Beam today; beam always.

Italy Comes with War and Chocolate

FOUR YEARS IN ITALY. This is what the military offered Ryan, and Ryan offered me, and together we sat stunned on his college apartment floor after he hung up the phone and wondered how on earth this chance was ours. We had expected his assignment to send us to some outer state, some barren corner that no one else wanted. But instead, it was: "We need a transportation officer in Italy who has your qualifications. Do you want the spot?"

Yes. Shout from the rooftops yes.

Three months after we got married, we packed our bags, our bikes, Ryan's maps, my novels.

We packed a car and sent it over on a ship.

Our families squeezed us tight before we left, told us how quickly they'd fly over to see us.

We rented the first floor of an Italian house because military housing was full—miraculously full—so we found a small rural town, a backdrop of mountains, a house with a beautiful gate. Our Italian landlords lived on the second floor above us, their daughter and grandson on the top, their son and his family in a house built directly behind. It was like a tiered cake—the layers of us inside, the flowers and vines circling the outside.

The floors were marble, even in the stairwells, and our landlords had lace tablecloths and polished heirlooms cased in glass cabinets. But all that grandeur was paired with broken and haphazard edges: falling down fences, old buckets and spilled wine, roaming chickens and dropped laundry soaking wet in the yard. I stood in our tiny kitchen next to Giovanna—our landlord—and learned to make wild strawberry jam, spiked milk, a proper coffee. She bossed us all around—the whole house of us, even Ryan in his starched uniform —and we just smiled and fell in line.

Our house was seven miles from the military post, so we often rode bikes or a motorcycle to and from. We knew every sharp turn and family pizzeria and fringed umbrella along the way. But even in the throes of all that beauty, there were deep shadows. Because life is life, after all, and no day is all one way or all the other.

We had lived there for a year when terrorists attacked New York City and horror hung in the skies, dropped a country to her knees.

Ryan and I were both on the military post but not together, and when I finally reached him, he said I needed to get home, all the families did. Homes were safer. And the soldiers would stay—the thousands who were trained and ready to get on an airplane and jump back out of it. Made ready for war, for support operations, for spontaneous departures. They knew what they had signed up for, and so did we.

"Go out the back gates. Use side exits," the families were told.

I heard the main entrance was already being blocked off with concrete barricades, barbed wire reinforcements. I followed the other families in a line of cars, but I don't remember driving home, just getting there.

Our landlords must have been away or asleep, their dogs and chickens out in the fields. The whole street was empty—in that air-sucked-out kind of way. I imagine it felt that way because everyone either knew what had just happened or was about to find out.

When I got inside our house, I pushed all my weight against the front door. It was the first time in two years I'd even turned the dead bolt. I dropped down the heavy metal shutters on every window and thought about anything else I could close down, lock tight. And while I wanted the dark house to feel safe and protected, it was the opposite. I felt trapped, my back against a wall. I couldn't see who was coming and going. We didn't have a TV at the house, didn't have Internet, and I realized that if I wasn't on the military post, I had no way of knowing what else was happening out there when it seemed, now, like anything could.

When I heard the buzzer pressed at our gate, the sound was jarring. For a while I sat on the floor next to the dark window, hoping it would stop, and whoever was there would give up. I couldn't imagine who would be coming to our house. You run through strange scenarios at times like these, when your body is on high alert, when you've been told to blend in so you aren't a target even though anyone could be.

But finally I unlocked the door and stepped out to see. It was a woman who lived down the street, her dark hair sweaty around her face, her face contorted in pain. She was holding a white box.

She started talking to me before I even had the gate open, asking me rapid questions in a language I hadn't yet learned, with her arms waving into the sky, pantomiming the attack. She started sobbing as she dropped her arms back down like she had no more to give. She slowed her words and started to use gestures to ask me: Was my husband safe? Are there more attacks coming? I said yes to the first, "Non lo so" to the second.

I wanted to sink to the ground; I was so exhausted and afraid. She told me about an American pilot who used to live on our street and how the neighbors all cared for him. She told me she liked us being on their street too. Then she held out the bent white box to me, lifted off the lid, and held it out. I looked at the rows of chocolate inside. Some were intact, but some had been taste tested, returned to the box.

It was hard to see straight. But I smiled at her offering, and she smiled back, stuck her hand into the box, and took one as if to show me what to do. So I chose one too. She tested hers and put it back in, which made me laugh. We finished our chocolate. Then she pulled me against her body and held me there, the box pushed out to the side of us. I put my forehead on her shoulder.

I wanted my family. I wanted Ryan to come home. I wanted to be back in my own country. But what I had was here, with an Italian stranger-neighbor in a sweaty housedress holding me, and I held her back.

Then she started to sing. She began softly, wandering across the low notes, then kept climbing higher and higher, letting them hang there in the September air. It was so vulnerable and unexpected that I lifted my head off her shoulder to watch her face. She closed her eyes and pressed on. The notes were off-key, fragile, extraordinary.

This woman had left her house and walked toward the place I was hiding. She came to find me and brought what she had in a white box. She came right away. Sometimes I imagine her getting halfway out her door but turning around to rummage in her cabinet to see what she had to offer before she came the rest of the way.

Sometimes the most beautiful hospitality looks like a box of half-eaten chocolate.

And it will land like a prayer.

Hospitality
with What You Have

Make a little extra coffee when you're brewing. Deliver it to a neighbor or someone working outside.

Offer to do a few loads of laundry for someone with little kids or an aging parent. Then set the basket of clothes, cleaned and folded, on their back porch without interrupting.

Invite a few people to join you for an outdoor dinner. Use what you have to set a table: an assortment of glassware, handmade name cards, a simple menu.

Remember what people say they love or would like to try. Surprise them with it.

SEND A FEW POSTCARDS TELLING PEOPLE WHAT THEY MEAN TO YOU AND HOW YOU BELIEVE IN THEM.

If someone drops something, looks lost, or seems stuck in another type of awkward situation, help them get out of it.

Give your phone number to your neighbors in case they ever have an emergency.

Invite someone to take a walk with you. Ask them what they're looking forward to these days.

Stick a quick, kind note under a stranger's windshield wiper.

Light candles before someone gets home or wakes up or visits.

Make one small, beautiful, and tidy scene, even if you're surrounded by wildness.

If a person seems left out or forgotten, stand or sit next to them. Don't call attention to yourself; just be there.

PLANT A GARDEN.

Give someone a bear hug. Nearly knock them off their feet.

Help a friend or sibling with a couple things on their to-do list; jump starts are huge gifts.

If someone is in pain, visit them, even if there's nothing to say.

Deliver a stack of firewood. Or a loaf of bread. Or a jar of honey.

Open and hold doors for others. Welcome them to a place even if it isn't yours.

Practice beaming.

Give someone your shoes or coat. It is good to walk away barefoot or coatless, at least once in our lives.

SHARE WHAT GROWS.

Coffee off the Stove, Apples, and Parm

01 Tamp your favorite coffee into your coffee maker. Use filtered water if available, for a cleaner taste. Turn on the stove and brew until sputtering and full.

02 Put some cream in a little pitcher and sugar in a bowl.

03 Thinly slice a crisp apple and find a wedge of salty cheese, such as Parmesan. Set them on a plate together.

04 If you have chocolate or cookies, tuck those onto the sides. Slices of cured meat are nice too. I like to fold them into waves.

05 Ask a thoughtful question as you drink and eat.

We picked up a stovetop coffee maker in Italy, but it seems they're all over the world now—and not expensive. They're little contraptions that sit on top of a burner, sputter when they're finished, and produce two tiny, charming cups of coffee that definitely make you feel you've crossed an ocean or stepped into a storybook to drink it.

When you have a guest, stovetop coffee also adds a touch of holiday—and with a plate of apples and cheese set between you, it becomes a little scene to gather around.

All Is Quiet in the Highlands

"STAY AS LONG AS YOU WANT," she said as she led me around the cabin.

Dusty poetry books were stacked on top of the potbelly stove. A small carton of eggs and a block of cheese were in the fridge. A fresh bar of soap was set on the tiled sill.

She flipped on a lamp, then turned down the mismatched covers on the bed next to the window. The quilt's edges were frayed; you felt their gentleness without even touching them. The whole cabin was soft, down to the cobwebs in the corners.

"Would you be able to stay here a little longer tonight?" I finally asked her, because while I wanted to spend a few days alone, I wasn't ready yet.

Solitude can be a fragile thing. You want it . . . but you have to ease into it so it doesn't overwhelm you. And I trusted her steady presence. She would not overload the space we had; she would just be in it.

So that night we sat on the rough-hewn porch of the slant-roof cabin until the sun set all the way, and then I slept like a lamb beside the front window under the frayed blankets, looking for stars and falling asleep that way, like she suggested.

In the morning, I was ready to be alone. I did some writing. I fried the eggs. I walked down to the water.

For years, I've collected these kinds of experiences—paid close attention to them—so I could understand what it was I wanted to offer to others. And what I've found is that gentleness is the umbrella: the thing that matters most. I want a place gentle enough that you can sit on floors and countertops and walk barefoot. I want a room gentle enough that you don't worry about how you'll be able to take care of it; it exists to take care of you. And I love a few provisions that are ready for you: a lamp by the bed, a few chosen books, pieces of fruit in a bowl, a coffeepot that isn't complicated.

And I want a host gentle enough that you can ask her for what you need—even if it's to stay with you for a few minutes longer in the evening on the porch, so you can ease yourself into the gift of uninterrupted space come morning.

Make a Guest Space

You don't need a separate, designated room to create a guest space. We didn't have one until this year; before, we used couches, a camper van, air mattresses in the basement. We've put our kids in one room to free up another. We've borrowed my parents' house and shuttled between. So don't be afraid of makeshift areas—just rearrange a little, add in some thoughtful items and elements, and extend the invite.

These are some of my favorite things to pull together for guests. But they are simply suggestions, and certainly not everything here is needed. Use what you have—and what you sense will make your guest feel comfortable and known.

a few thoughtfully chosen books
a candle and matches
a new toothbrush just in case
an extra roll of toilet paper
a well-folded stack of towels
a fresh bar of soap
full bottles of shampoo and conditioner
a blanket for taking outside
a pen and paper
something fresh (branches, flowers, herbs) in a cup or vase
eggs, a pastry or a half-loaf of bread, butter, honey, whole fruit
coffee and a coffee maker
tea and a kettle
cream and sugar
a small simple gift or welcome note

Ease your hospitality efforts and make it all more sustainable by generally repeating the same setup each time. Then you have go-to elements established so you're not going back to the drawing board each time. If you have an empty drawer or storage spot, you can bundle these things together and pull them out when it's time.

Don't wait until everything is seemingly perfect or ready. Invite anyway.

Sibyl Gave Me a Bicycle

MY FRIEND DIED WHEN SHE WAS TEN, riding her bike down a hill, hit by a car at the bottom. My other friend called me to say Whitney is gone. I hung up the phone and pretended it hadn't happened. I went down to dinner with a straight face. My parents found out later from other parents, and they came to tell me again what had happened to Whitney. I climbed into the back of my closet to cry.

A few days later, a woman named Sibyl delivered a golden bicycle necklace to our house. Sibyl was a constant in my life: she had created a huge youth camp where all my sisters and I went in the summers. That's where we learned how to shoot a bow and arrow, check for ticks, sleep in old cabins in the dead heat of summer, meet God at the water.

Our family would go to Sibyl's house on Sundays. In her kitchen, we would dip a wooden spoon into the honey jar, listen to people read from good books and the Bible, then run through her garden always full of tomatoes and strawberries. Sibyl knew how to inspire us, magnify us, kneel gently at our level.

But when she brought me the bike necklace, my fury rose like a storm.

I wanted to be alone and run from my sadness. I had no plan to face it; I had learned the art of dissociation and was well practiced. So after she left, I dug a hole in the backyard and dropped the necklace into a white jewelry box, pushed it all into the ground with my foot.

Sometimes I'd think about it out there, a little tomb. I never dug it up, and when we moved away from that childhood house, I knew it was still there like an unwanted pearl in the black earth.

It took thirty-five years to want the necklace back.

It took forty years to understand why Sibyl gave me what felt to be the exact wrong thing. Except it was the right thing, because she knew me. She knew my tendency and defenses; I think she understood I was trying to outrun my pain and wanted to help me experience that horrible grief so it wouldn't erupt in other ways, as unfelt grief will do. Sibyl wanted to help me look at what happened without pushing it down, and without leaving me alone.

Eventually, I got there.

The bicycle necklace is still buried in the backyard of my childhood home, but I finally feel like I'm starting to wear it: I miss my friend Whitney. I wish she hadn't died. She was funny and loud, and she would cartwheel with me across the middle school playground even though we were the only ones, and we were wearing uniform skirts. We'd run back to class at the very last second, our hair all fuzzed and knotted, our knees speckled with asphalt, because Whitney always insisted we take things a little too far.

IS THERE ANYTHING YOU'VE
BURIED THAT YOU'RE
READY TO FACE?

ARE YOU A SAFE PLACE
FOR OTHERS TO DO THEIR
UNBURYING WORK?

Not the Saviors Here

I HAVE DONE A LOT OF OVERSERVING.
I've put others' needs too far in front of my own and even my family's. I've gotten too deep into the emotional needs of people I shouldn't have. And then I've backed myself into corners with no capacity or guardrails in place for people who thought I could "be everything" to them when I was never meant to be.

We are not the full rescue. We are not the saviors here.

But when you're wired toward hospitality and caretaking, you may slide into these missing-boundary waters if you're not aware of your effect on others' hearts and also your own.

I imagine we get to this position in different ways—and some are very well intentioned. But some of that motivation may actually come from an unhealthy need to be the one everyone else can depend on. The one everyone can *really* count on, lean on, cry on . . . so then you are also the one who's most needed. This can feel like an honor and a reward, but it isn't sustainable—and it isn't good for anyone involved.

You can serve and love people calmly. Every person around you shouldn't get the same level of emotional connection or the same invitation into your personal spaces. And I've learned it's also serving others in the larger sense by respecting their boundaries, even if they aren't holding them on their own.

Finding this balance isn't always simple. It relies on your instinct and integrity. If you pay attention, you usually sense when you're about to cross a line or give too much. You'll often know when your motivation is off-key or when you've been vying for hero status and gotten in your own way. If you have a hard time seeing this type of thing on your own, ask a good and healthy mentor to help you discern along the way.

Sibyl gave me a bicycle necklace, but she also gave me space. Years of it. She didn't do the hardest work for me—she thoughtfully offered a direction and let me decide if I would take it. This takes a great deal of self-control. It moves you out of the rescuer spot entirely. It allows the ones you're loving and hosting in your life to grow forward, not get knotted around your neck.

You may bend forward and backward a little, as life and people come at you, but you buoy back into that standing position. Because you know who you are, what you have to offer, and what you don't or can't.

You are grounded and gentle and safe—not a hero, not God.

Two People in the Grocery Store

THE CODE CAME OVER THE LOUDSPEAKER of the grocery store. It was a code I knew from times before: when you hear a number called out plus the aisle location, it seems to mean there's a person in the store who the manager has an eye on.

There's a man who rides his bike to the grocery, up and down a well-trafficked street. He wears plastic bags over his hands when it's cold, and he has a basket attached to his bike where he seems to store his food and long pieces of cardboard. His hair and beard are long, white. I don't know where he lives, just the street he rides on.

When I heard the grocery store code announced over the loudspeaker and saw the white-bearded man from a distance, I figured the code was for him. He had one of the store's carts and a few things inside.

But a woman in a nurse's uniform was the first to appear. She went right next to him, leaned close, and spoke quietly. She smiled and gestured toward the produce he had in the corner of his cart. He said something back. Then she got cash out of her wallet. He took it and smiled. She slowly trailed him to the checkout, picking up things for her own cart along the way.

I passed him on my way home, pedaling down the street, basket full of the gifted produce.

This was years ago, and I still think about it. I think about how they went shoulder to shoulder in the store that day. How they made it work quietly: a small offering and receiving, then they both headed home.

WAYS TO SHOW HOSPITALITY AWAY FROM HOME

hand out cold water on hot days

pay someone's way

help carry something when a person is struggling

offer to let someone go in front of you

hold the door open

pick up what's been dropped

make eye contact and smile a greeting

deliver a simple breakfast

compliment a stranger

Dad Gave It Away

ONE DAY I CAME HOME FROM SCHOOL, AND MY DOLLHOUSE WAS GONE. All the furniture and figurines, all the little scenes I'd set up inside. I was standing in our basement play area looking at the vacant spot when my sister came rushing down and told me that a family my dad worked with had a terrible fire and their whole house had burned down. Their kids lost everything, she said—even their backpacks. They lost their toys too, she said, while noticing what I had noticed. Later my dad came home and told us what else we could do to help them. We went to our rooms and sorted through all our drawers.

I don't remember minding after I heard what had happened. My dad still feels awful, says he wishes he had asked us first and let us be part of the decision. But we don't always do generosity perfectly, and sometimes it's a sacrifice you aren't expecting. I still think what he did was beautiful. A dollhouse is replaceable. I loved having it, but I also loved that we had something to give.

And it made sense to me—it didn't really catch me off guard—because for my whole life, my dad has been giving things away. Taking care of needs. Anonymously paying someone's way. Donating what they still used but believed someone else needed more.

I hear stories all the time:

He gave me his car.
He paid my bill.
He saved my business.
He put air in my tires when I parked on his driveway.
He called to make sure I got home okay.

Sometimes it's something big. And sometimes it's a dollhouse, because you're trying to lift anything you can from the ashes.

Make Hospitality Bags

We used to keep paper bags filled with a few supplies in the back of our van. So when people asked us for money at traffic lights, we would ask if they wanted a few extra things too. These are some of the items we put in the bags, but depending on the season and state you live in and what you have, you can include whatever items you think best.

whole piece of fruit
protein bar
bottle of water
pack of gum
new socks
gloves
hand sanitizer
cash
a deck of cards
a pen and small notebook

I used to feel awkward talking about giving things to people in need. I didn't know if our family was doing it well or giving the right things or interfering with something in the bigger picture. But when we handed out these bags, every person seemed glad to receive them. And I figure if there's something they don't need in the bag, they might give it to someone else.

If there's a better way to quickly offer a small gift to others who are asking for help, maybe I'll hear about it. But until then, it's time for us to restock the van and remember to spread goodwill, even in the smallest of ways.

Returning What's Been Lost

IT WAS A SUMMER DAY, AND MY MOM WALKED ME TO THE BAKERY. It had to have been a few miles away from our house, and I'm not sure how she had the time to do this in the middle of the afternoon. Our family was big, and she was working at the time. But we slowly walked together to the little blue bakery in the old part of town where the screen door was so lightweight it nearly bounced off when you opened it. And inside, the long row of glass-front cases. The little cakes with pale icing, the white paper doilies, the cursive handwritten labels. I picked out my pastry. My mom got her Styrofoam cup of coffee.

We started walking home, keeping an eye out for where to sit and eat. We chose a stump by a stop sign, probably because I couldn't wait any longer. And while we were having our bakery picnic, I spotted a piece of grass near us that must have been missed by the city's lawnmower. It stood tall above the rest, and my mom says she remembers I felt sorry for it. So I asked her if I could take it home. I picked the blade and set it next to me on the stump while I ate.

But then I left the blade of grass there, distracted by other things I'm sure, and didn't realize what had happened until we got all the way back home and walked in the front door and my hands were empty. I told my mom what happened with tears. And without hesitating, she got her car keys and drove back to the spot where I'd left it. She brought it home, and I put it in a glass of water on the kitchen sill.

I think now about how significant this recovery was to me—in all its childhood simplicity—because my mom taught me that we can love people by helping them retrieve what's been left behind or lost.

Sometimes we lose our way back home.

Sometimes we lose our nerve.

Sometimes we lose our ability to get from A to Z.

Sometimes we lose a friend.

Sometimes we simply lose a blade of grass.

And when our legs are too tired to return to those things ourselves, or when we can't figure out how we're going to get them back, we might need someone to step in, get their car keys, and help us bring the lost things home.

Little Cakes*

Serve these little cakes for dessert or breakfast, pack them up for a road snack, or surprise a neighbor with a few wrapped in parchment and tied with string.

01 Preheat oven to 350°F. Bring all cold ingredients—butter, eggs, and buttermilk—to room temperature.

02 Grease your pan with shortening. Use whatever pan style you want: Bundt, mini Bundt, cupcake, loaf. (The size you choose will alter how long you leave it in the oven.)

03 In a stand mixer or with a hand mixer, beat shortening and butter at medium speed for one minute. Gradually add sugar, beating until light, fluffy, and pale yellow. This takes at least five minutes. But don't overmix the batter, or it will affect the texture and prevent your cakes from rising.

04 Add the lemon and vanilla extracts.

05 Add eggs, one at a time, beating just until the yolk disappears after each addition.

06 In a separate bowl, whisk the flour, baking powder, and salt. With the mixer on the lowest speed, gradually add half of the flour mixture to the creamed mixture.

07 Add the buttermilk to the creamed mixture, and then add the rest of the flour mixture, continuing to mix at low speed until combined.

08 Pour batter into the greased pan and bake at 350°F for 20–40 minutes (depending on your pan size) until a toothpick comes out clean. Cool in the pan on a cooling rack to let it settle.

09 Top with icing glaze, powdered sugar, lemon shavings, berries, whipped cream—whatever looks lovely to you.

1 cup salted butter

5 eggs

1¼ cups buttermilk

½ cup butter-flavored shortening (plus extra to grease pan)

3 cups sugar

3 cups all-purpose flour

2 teaspoons baking powder

1 teaspoon salt

2 teaspoons lemon extract (or more, to taste)

1 tablespoon pure vanilla extract

toppings (optional)

* Recipe contributed by Nickey Stevenson.

PART 2

breaking
GROUND

Land

STICKS BREAKING UNDERFOOT. This is a sound I connect, now, with a dream rising above the surface. It's the sound of us pulling back branches, stepping over old roots, and finally saying out loud, "This is the place. This is where we want to build a house."

The first time Ryan and I walked the hillside, we felt it in our bones—the unusual peace it seemed to hold, the hint of promise, the set-apart quiet we longed to settle into.

We had planned and saved for twenty-two years. We had lived overseas and come back again, worked jobs from the ground up, left them, and returned to them. We had spoken dreams out loud and driven toward them.

Family. Land. The making of a new haven.

We had so many maps and design magazines dog-eared and circled that our paper trail was longer than a highway. For decades, we picked up pieces of things we loved and set them along windowsills: oyster shells, acorns, ceramic tiles, paint samples. We took photos, gathered materials, underlined architects' names. We drew floor plans and house outlines. We stayed up late, sketching the long and low shape of a house, a gravel courtyard, a stone wall to sit on.

We filled our pockets with ideas from Italy. California. New Hampshire.

We noted the color of tree bark, town *pasticcerias*, fringe umbrellas on the coast.

We pulled inspiration from book illustrations, cabin visits, the homes of our grandparents.

And during all that drawing and dreaming, we rented a stream of lackluster places. We didn't mind too much, because we imagined others, and we were thankful to have places to live at all. We set up temporary homes in apartments and government rentals. My sister's attic. An extended-stay hotel.

I knew a good home could crop out of any sort of shelter; I knew it didn't rely on great floor plans or charming metal roofs. Even our most forlorn places usually held dashes of hope, and we figured out ways to make little scenes despite the bland walls or government furniture, small attempts to create pockets of beauty in unlikely places.

I started relying on natural light and removing all the shades and blinds I could. I decorated with stacks of books, since I had those in abundance, and brought leafy branches inside when flowers weren't around. We tried to balance out the vinyl and laminate surfaces by adding extra rugs, stacks of blankets, glass cups, wood trays, big bowls of fruit.

Some of our living arrangements worked better than others. Sometimes the fleas that come with your rented furniture will sink your spirit and make you want to run for the hills, or at least live in your parents' house again. But we kept up our hopes for a future landing. We kept adding to the windowsill collection with tile samples, buttons and brass knobs, shells that felt like just the right color for a bedroom wall.

We lucked out wildly with our rental house in Italy, but after that it was back to another attic apartment for art school, and then a year when I lived back at my parents' house while Ryan was

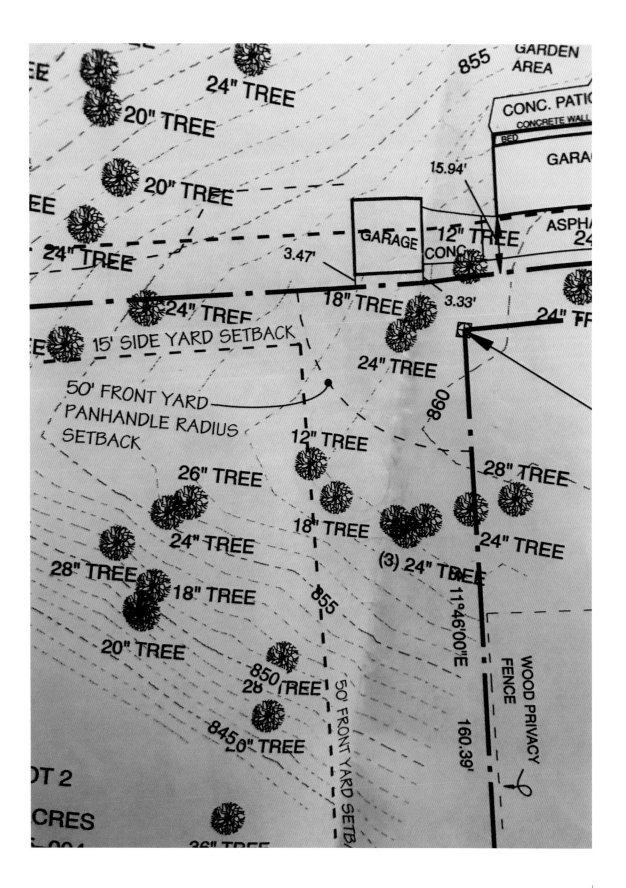

deployed during the war in the Middle East. While he was in the desert, I walked around the city between university classes, dreaming about where we could live one day. I wanted to paint walls we wouldn't leave, plant rosemary in the ground instead of in pots, send holiday cards with a permanent return address stamped in the corner.

After a year and a half, Ryan came home. He was finished with his military duty and I was finished with grad school, and in so many ways it was like starting anew. We found a small midcentury house that an elderly artist was selling, and as soon as she opened the aqua front door—with a bookshelf backlit behind her and a stretch of windows looking out on trees—my heart soared. I saw the same look in Ryan's eyes: we had found it. Even though it needed mountains of work that we probably didn't have time or skill for, and even though we had so much to learn about what it means to own a house and bear this new responsibility, we were ready. We bartered with family members who were skilled in construction and began the renovation.

We could finally plant rosemary. We could paint walls.

And then, after eight years of marriage, we had our first baby. Then in a couple years another, then another. It was happening—this movement into parenthood—and the profound gift of it was not lost on us. We were building the second half of our lives.

My three sisters had babies too, lots of them, so we grew into this rambling crowd of cousins and kinships, trying to figure out what it means to live alongside one another, forgive the missteps, attempt boundaries, and work through the highs and lows of being a group of people so woven together because we are sisters raised to believe family comes first—but suddenly our family was spilling over the edges with husbands and babies and in-laws, and that's a lot of family to come first.

We began opening the door to more and more people.

I had started a magazine in my off hours—those hours sporadically found in the midst of a career and building a family. And since creative endeavors can fill me with such energy, even in the middle of the night, after nursing a baby, I would fall back asleep taking notes in my head for what essay went on which page, what photograph would be on the cover, how I would pitch the product to stores for distribution. And just when I needed the extra hands and skill sets, a group of young women in the throes of design school began visiting our house. They had heard about the magazine; they knocked on the door.

They were surprisingly drawn to a place where toddlers and a newborn, book drafts and espresso cups, photographs and mood boards were all piled and gathered around the same table. They didn't mind tantrums or tears or conversations that were cut off until I could get one of our children to sleep. They showed grace and offered help. We were in vastly different phases of life, but maybe that's exactly why it worked.

This overlapping of work and mothering and dream-pursuit came with sacrifice and tensions to sort through, but I was willing. I had spoken the truth in art school. I didn't need everything, but I knew I could not be a singularly focused person. I have no desire to be a solitary novelist. I want to be right in the middle of all my people, heart full and available, hands designing books but also packing lunches. So on some days I worked, and some mornings I wrote, then on other days Ryan and I would drive our kids to a farm and pick blueberries and eat cider doughnuts. I'd spend hours with them in parks and sand pits, squeezing their sticky, wonderful hands as we crossed streets and followed puppies or the funny shadows that caught their eyes.

I wanted to be a mom like my mom, letting them collect blades of grass and build forts out of sheets and make breakfast together, even if eggshells ended up in the omelets.

When our family of five outgrew the house with the aqua door and college visitors, we had the chance to move onto a street right next to two of my sisters, and it felt exactly right exactly then. It was a solid suburban home that didn't inspire us by any stretch, but it was a simple house that we didn't have to fix or worry about, and that's a beautiful thing when you're raising a young family. So our kids got to grow up next door to their cousins, which meant years of open garage doors, sharing lawnmowers and ideas, dragging the lemonade stand in and out, borrowing sugar and dinners and energy when your own fell flat.

It wasn't easy to add more people to the mix in those years (just like it still isn't, sometimes), so we didn't pull it off often. But I took Sibyl's advice to let hospitality become more natural, more of an "offer what you have . . . even if you wish it could be more." The reality was, we couldn't pull off gorgeous dinner parties or promise a quiet house in the mornings or spend hours in conversation focused on guests. It was hard for me to let go of these ideals. But we figured out what we could do. We could rearrange bedrooms and make a little space. We could invite our guests to listen to bedtime stories or throw the football with us. We could set a platter of pretty, simple food on the small countertop and eat on the floor when we ran out of seats.

At night, Ryan and I sat in folding chairs on our concrete driveway with chalk drawings scribbled around our feet, and we knew the gift of it—to have a good house and live next to family. We figured even if sometimes the wheels were half falling off, at least we were still upright and trying to love one another and sitting in the center of chalk flowers and balloons.

Many times, we wondered if it was selfish to want anything different from what we had. We wondered if some dreams don't need to be clung to. But still, we couldn't shake the idea that one day we wanted to build from the ground up. Have a little more space. Have wider doors.

The new property is shaped like a wedge of pie. It sits along the bottom rim of Ohio on a hillside that flattens at the top and flattens again at the bottom.

My parents bought the land years ago from retired maple syrup farmers who barely wanted to let it go, and we all understood why. It's tucked back a couple of hundred feet off a main road. Private but not far away. A minute after turning out of the driveway, you're next to gas stations and traffic and Taco Bell. So it's woodsy but not isolated. And it's adjacent to my parents' home and oldest sister's farmhouse: three properties in a hilly row. My other two sisters and their families are still only five minutes away.

"You could bank the house right there," my dad said, pointing, standing at the top of the pie, and it's hard not to picture it. We see a house that could be close to the ground and ramble across the top, be settled between the oaks and redbuds.

But we would have to leave the house on the street with two of my sisters and their families, and I worried I would never stop grieving this part of it. I wanted all of us together always; I wanted five houses in a hilly row, but that just wasn't how it unfolded. And I knew it was all so unusual anyway—for families to live as neighbors. Some people thought it was crazy; some teased about the compound we'd created; some said they had similar dreams for their own families, and we told them how many years it took to get here.

You also come to realize that every choice means something else isn't chosen. If we chose to build here, we weren't choosing there. If we chose to live in Ohio, we weren't choosing to go back to Italy. If we chose a house on a wooded hill, we weren't choosing a place where we could have lemonade stands on a quiet neighborhood street where my brother-in-law came and dropped way too much cash in the tip jar and filled the curbside crew with glee.

But finally we did choose. After twenty-two years of imagining, collecting, preparing, we handed all our sketches and ideas to an architect, staked it out, then found a builder to dig the hole and make it real. We watched the explosion of dust and wood chips, the delivery of metal and pipe, the unboxing of tile the color of an Italian grotto we once swam underneath.

While half of the days I marveled over it and embraced it fully, I also hit rough waves of doubt, guilt, fear. Because now it was becoming real, and real is a lot to swallow. While I had grown accustomed to risk in the creative world—building a house was like pushing all our chips to the center of the table. My fear grew like vines.

Sometimes it feels terrifying to land—to stop in your tracks, drop your bags, and say, "*Here.*"

I was afraid of choosing poorly. I was afraid of committing to the wrong dream, locking in to a plan that might or might not be the best one. I was afraid the choice was too big, too weighty to bear in the end. I was afraid our kids wouldn't feel at home in a new house, wouldn't like their new rooms, would cry quietly in the middle of the night—and it would be our fault.

MICHAEL ONDAAT

FM 3-05.70 SURVIVAL

FM 7-8 INFANTRY RIFLE PLATOON AND SQUAD

JAMES WASHINGTON SQUARE

I was afraid I didn't deserve to build a new house and that other people might think the same. I was afraid of messing something up. And I hated all this fear; I was embarrassed by it and still am. I want to be strong and steady. I don't want to second-guess, because waffling feels like chaos, and I just want peace.

When I felt the vines get tight, I tried looking the other way, distracting myself with tile colors and roof angles, but it didn't always work. I don't think you can outrun fear that way. I needed to understand where the vines were coming from and ask for help with the weed whacker.

Before we bought the property, my friend Jennie and I were asked to design an overnight camping experience for women. Our church was still growing and eager—and after a camp for the men was started, it became clear that the women wanted one too. So we spent the next few years guiding women into open fields and tree lines, offering them room for adventure and rest.

One night, after restocking firewood and toilet paper, I sat under a big white tent we called the prayer tent—filled with a bunch of hay bales and women ready to care for one another, to get still and listen for God. It was a well-visited place, and we'd have a line of women winding all the way down the hill as they waited for the next open hay bale. It would start in the morning and stretch past dark.

Everyone went to the line, even if we were there as leaders.

"It's like I can't stop running," a tall woman said to me, her eyes down. "Even the thought of slowing down makes me panic."

She shifted on the hay bale, pulled back.

I could feel the rise in my own pulse, recognizing similar patterns in my own life. "I think I know what you mean," I said, trying not to over-relate. "It can feel really good to run." She looked up.

"I think running feels easier somehow."

I nodded. Then she told me a little about her days, her duties, the things she was avoiding.

"What do you think would happen if you stopped running?" I asked.

This was close to home, and I needed to learn something too.

"I think I'd basically die if I stopped." She laughed, but then her voice lowered. "I think I'd find out, maybe . . . I'm wasting my time here?" she said. "Like the stuff I'm doing with my life—what if all of it doesn't really amount to much? I don't know if I could handle facing that."

Maybe we both realized the same thing at the same time: that running and movement can feel a lot like protection. Running keeps us from being rejected by others or seeing disappointment or feeling defeated. So we often stay busy on the surface, skimboarding through life, running away or in circles. We distract ourselves with tile colors and roof angles.

I looked around at the crowd of women inside the prayer tent and figured a lot of us were running in one way or another. Running as a way to avoid a reality we're living in. Running as a way to reject before we get rejected. Running as a way to protect our hearts when commitment seems too high a cost or when we're afraid to make a choice and stick to it. It's strange how running can feel like freedom, even when it isn't.

I looked back at her.

"But right now . . . it seems like you're not running, and you're doing okay so far?"

She lifted an eyebrow and smiled. "I guess so."

"Maybe facing what's in front of us isn't going to be as terrible as it seems."

"Maybe not."

I wanted to convince myself too.

"But I guess it could be hard or uncomfortable."

"Yeah . . . I might decide I need to change something. But then at least I'd know. At least I could see around me a little better, instead of flying past it."

We both nodded; we knew she was right.

In the distance, someone was ringing the bell for dinner. It was an old bell hanging off an old tree that must have been there for decades, calling people toward one another, calling us to stop and sit.

Under the dinner tent, I could see volunteers lighting candles, setting out the handwritten name cards, filling drinks. A few musicians were testing their microphones, then settling into their notes and voices.

I have needed and still need people to remind me what it means to stop and get steady. I need friends and sisters and a husband who know my ins and outs, who know my tendency to chuck things out the window or run like the wind when I don't know how else to handle my fear or nerves. I need people to reach out, hold on to me, and say, "It's okay to stop here. It's okay to stay in place and stop making excuses or distractions. It's okay to look at things directly."

The old bell kept ringing. The dinner tent was filling up.

"Want to race to dinner?" I shrugged dramatically, hoping she would get the joke.

To my relief, she laughed.

We had landed, and we were okay.

"Can we walk away from it?" I asked Ryan one night.

The house was nearly finished, nearly ready to hold us. Tomorrow, they were painting and installing doorknobs. The vines of fear were tightening.

"Should we just sell it before we move in?"

Ryan looked at me and was quiet for a while. I think I've shown him every fault and fear card by this point, and even if I throw him for a loop, he usually ends up taking it in stride. But there we were, elbows deep into the biggest thing we'd ever invested in, elbows deep in something we cared deeply about and had collaborated on for so many years, and I was getting cold feet every other night in the kitchen and saying things like, "Let's bail."

And Ryan isn't a new friend on a hay bale at camp I may never see again.

"Yes . . . we *can* walk away from this. If you're this troubled by it, and if this is going to be how it keeps making you feel and how it's going to affect all of us . . . going back and forth over whether we made the right choice . . . then we can stop. We can sell it. It isn't worth it, for any of us."

"Really?"

"Yes."

"Do you think it's a good idea to give it up?"

"No, I don't."

I walked across the kitchen to Ryan and buried my face in his chest.

"I'm sorry, Ry. Maybe it'll be okay after all."

I glanced up at him. He was lifting an eyebrow in mock annoyance, and I rolled my eyes back at him.

He is my favorite. He doesn't run when I run; he reaches for my hand.

Yes. It can be hard to land.

To make a decision and hold steady.

To choose one thing and not the other.

To stop skimming the surfaces so you can see where you are.

To believe that right here is a place worth tending.

To start with today.

And take space when you stop.

We are worth the space we take when we stop. Our lives are worth looking at, being thoughtful about, being tended to. We are worth the time it takes to work through fear, as many times as it crops up. We are worth joining hands with. And as we do this foundational landing work, we learn what it means to be at home, to be present and comfortable with all parts of ourselves, vines and all. We are anchored by honesty. And this way of landing gives others around us permission to do the same.

Practice Landings

Realize that no place, no land, no person, no community is without flaw.

Realize that you cannot be perfect or atone for all your mistakes or make everyone happy.

Lay on the ground one afternoon. In the sun, if you can. Let your mind settle.

Tell someone soon why you think you've been on the run—and what from.

Decide where you want to stop and get steady.

Write those landings on this page if you want to.

Keep the promises you make to yourself.

Give grace to other runners.

Give grace to yourself as you learn to take root.

SPACE TO LAND

Tents, Carts, Conversations— and All the Havens in Between

WE BROUGHT GRASS INSIDE THE WARE-HOUSE—rolls and rolls of it. We spread it out on the huge concrete floor like a dark field, misted water over it in the early morning before the building opened, tried to keep it fresh and soft for what was about to happen.

We were building an installation for the church: a place anyone who wanted to could step in, move at their own pace, and quietly interact with an experience that was designed for letting go of burdens and finding what had been lost. It was called *The Journey Home*.

We brought in chopped firewood and rocks and a hundred white canvas tents. We painted signs to lead people through. We sourced a whole slew of thrifted suitcases, still with their travel stickers and tags, and piled them on one side of the warehouse where people could pick one up. Eventually, as the guests wound their way from spot to spot, they would sit next to their suitcase and write on it.

"What do you want to let go of in your life? What are you finished with?"

They wrote their burdens in black marker across the vinyl and leather cases. They wrote everywhere: on the tags, under the seams, even across the zippers when their burdens ran longer than expected.

One day a man fell asleep in one of the tents. Maybe he fell asleep because he'd finally let go of something that had over-gripped his heart, and releasing it was so powerful that even in a faux camp space with hundreds of people moving around him, he needed to close his eyes. Or maybe he was just tired from a long day's work.

After an experience like this, you hear a lot of stories. Many of us bottle up and block our burdens so well, or we run so habitually, that when we get permission to unearth stuff that has been heavily guarded, we almost tip over once we release it. We can even fall asleep in public.

Since that installation, I've tried to build off that experience, but mostly it comes in small or spontaneous ways. I began recognizing that building havens for people can take any number of shapes, sizes, time frames. You don't have to bring sod and suitcases into a warehouse; you just consider how to surround others with permission and kindness, even if it's momentary. Even if it just offers a glimpse of how much each of us matters, here.

A hot coffee into cold hands.

An invitation on a lonely holiday.

An offer of help in a moment of overwhelm.

The other day I was standing in a long checkout line at a store holding too many things. I was sweating and exhausted after days of packing boxes and loading trucks, and since I'm not great at planning what I need before I go into a store, I skip a cart half the time but always need one in the end. My hands were full. A woman in front of me left her place in line and came back to me pushing a cart. She slid it under the load I was carrying and said, "I thought you could use this."

I was so caught off guard—so relieved to be taken care of by a stranger to whom I had nothing to give in return—that I'm still thinking about it. I wasn't a typical "help case." Not pregnant, not on crutches, not asking. Just sweating. And still she left her place in line to make mine better.

Maybe you have chances in your work or your life to create big or significant experiences for others, or maybe you have a guest space in your home to bring in the weary, or maybe you have time to write letters or start conversations that lift hearts. No matter what you have, you can probably get out of line at the grocery store and love your neighbor.

Havens can be

temporary, like a tent
permanent, like a house
momentary, like helping a stranger in line
lasting, like deep work in a community
shared around a table
shared within a story
felt in the space you give someone to take a nap
felt in the way you let someone speak without
*   interruption*
the way you lift burdens out of someone's hands
the way you hold someone close and beam in their
*   presence*

Building havens doesn't hinge on resources; it's
taking care of one another even in the simplest of
ways. It's hospitality with what you have.

come inside

you are welcome here
come in from the cold
come in from the heat

these walls will embrace you,
this ground is forgiving,
the ceiling carries your prayers
straight where they belong

home is no elusive concept here
home is here

the weight of the all behind you
leave at the door
as you make your way to
the table

the menu is truth and love
we will be ever clear about this

honesty and care,
we will see you

the light is on, for you
the fire blazes, for you
there's a rest here for you

come and be known
come inside
this is home
because you're here

ENIOLA ABIOYE

To Start: 11×17

I FOUND THEM STACKED NEAR ME AT WORK: large, exquisitely empty sheets of paper. They were white and crisp like printer paper, but one wonderful size bigger.

When I started doing my work on them, I realized how much I crave that kind of space to map things out—whether it's an event timeline, a magazine design, a room layout, or a map of my current life. The standard 8½×11-inch papers never seem to hold enough space for me, no matter which way I turn them or how small I write and draw. And poster size just overwhelms me. But 11×17s? The loveliest.

They give you all the room you need for words and sketches to spread themselves out. Then you still have plenty of space to add circles and arrows and revisions—with room to grow as your ideas keep radiating and turning corners.

In the past few years, I've slowly been sliding 11×17 sheets to my sisters and friends. I whisper, "Want to try this too?" I'm not an evangelist, just a paper pusher.

So when you think about breaking ground—whether it's building something new, planning an experience, or refreshing what you have—I believe it will bring you a dose of freedom to take it out of that idea-in-your-head realm and bring it down to the concreteness of a big piece of paper. Settle those swirling parts and pieces. Find your starting point. See how it could all come together.

I use 11×17 for things like these:

DESIGN MAP

When I'm starting from scratch (with a mound of dirt, an empty room, a storyline), it's hard to get a real sense of something unless I lay it out. Even if you're not an artist, try sketching. The shapes can be really basic, but even basic shapes have a way of revealing what the elements need to be. Then add words to describe what you're drawing. And don't be afraid to revise after you see what fits and what doesn't. Paper is still pretty cheap. Recycle and move on.

EXPERIENCE OR EVENT MAP

Whether I'm designing a single event or some kind of bigger experience for people, the sequence is really important to plan out, even just in a general-flow sense. I want to imagine and think about the moment-by-moment experience my guests will have—from how they'll enter the space to where they'll set their things or pick something up. Will there be music for ambiance? Something to look at when time is idle? A place to run a little wild? By mapping it out, I also see where a note or sign would be helpful, where it would be good to have another person leading the way, and where a rest stop could be a relief.

LIFE MAP

Every year or two I get out a blank 11×17 and start mapping the parts of my life and our family's life—a few words to represent each thing. Building a house. The kids' schooling. A big work project. A new dream. A short list of people who are significant in our lives. I start with the biggest elements and circle them. Then I add in the little things that are important but not as big. I draw boxes around things I want to focus on, write down some big-picture notes, add some sketches to help it sink in.

Making one of these life maps is grounding. It lets you look at what's happening right around you and what you're actually investing in (or not). You see the places and the people you're putting your time into. You notice if there's a gaping hole around hobbies, fresh adventure, breaks from work. Then you can look directly at what you have, what you want to let go of, how you want to grow.

You can also use 11×17s for placemats, lemonade stand signs, fire starters.

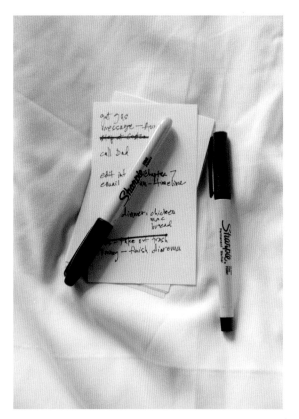

Then: Index Cards

AFTER MAPS AND BIG PICTURES, I love to get down to the brass tacks. Because if I don't have daily executions to follow, I'm a puddle of what-now. So I'm a big believer in arranging each day, from the morning forward. I make my day's list on an index card. It's a size that fits in a pocket or a cupholder and has enough thickness to stand up on its own, so it won't fall apart as it travels with me from van to desk to backyard on repeat.

But I don't overfill my index cards; I make them very doable. Because if you're in the throes of big work, which we all are, you know it's not help-ful to put "write a book" or "plant a garden" on your to-do list. That'll probably sink you. It's way better to jot down "draft the beginning of chapter 10" or "buy seedlings." Much gentler, much more productive.

Index card lists have also really helped me as a young mother. I don't do well if my days feel like I'm not sure where they started, what I did, and how I moved the needle forward. A little list on an index card is my mark of movement. It's a guide-post that settles the blur that day, even if my tasks often look the same.

I pull the index card out throughout the day; my memory is not enough. And I always cross out an item when I'm finished (I adore that part). If I don't finish everything on the index card, it's okay and normal. I keep the index card until the next morning, and anything I didn't do (that I still think is important), I carry forward and write on the new card.

Get a pack of blank index cards—or lined ones, if you like lines.

Each day, create a reasonable, actionable, not-too-long list.

Include nice things too, like "get root beer floats." Because it definitely helps to include nice things.

Add chores that you're going to do anyway. It's so fun to cross those out.

Sometimes, add something you're going to do for someone else.

And sometimes, add something that moves your 11×17 vision forward.

Then cross out whatever you finish when you finish it.

Didn't do it all? No big deal. Carry it forward, if it's still important.

But here's the thing: if these daily cards don't bring you peace, drop the practice.

Rolls of Paper and Sacrificial Content

"KILL YOUR DARLINGS" is what my writing professor called it—and I believe it holds up as good advice for how to create anything new, how to get something from start to finish, how to collaborate with others.

The darlings are like those lines of a story you began with or the vision you started with or the first way you set the furniture in a room when you unpacked. But maybe you sense something isn't quite working (or you get feedback from someone else that it isn't), except you can't bear to let those early precious things go. You keep forcing tiny shoes back onto bigger feet.

I've watched lots of people refuse to let go of darlings, and I've hung tight myself. While it may be wise to hold close to a vision, I haven't seen wisdom in restricting adjustments or being unwilling to listen to or integrate others' suggestions.

I've learned, whether I'm writing a story or building a house or designing an experience, it's important to start—right out of the gate—by understanding it is a draft. It is not unyielding. "Wet cement," you might call it, or "sacrificial content."

When I put something on paper or pitch it to a work team, I know it could get swapped for a new version. I remind myself that nothing I create should be too precious to shake loose a bit. And if you're creating or making things with other people, you will be a much better partner when you go after work this way. It's very hard to create with territorial, defensive folks.

Whether you're leading or following, be a safe person to brainstorm with and give feedback to. It helps to keep a calm face as you listen so you don't shut down the collaboration. Pay attention and give value to what others say. Then decide how and if you'll adapt.

Approaching creative work this way also helps me get something down in the first place— because I know it doesn't need to be perfect or exact. Anne Lamott is a brilliant teacher of this (read *Bird by Bird* if you like to write, and you will be in heaven). The willingness to put down a draft helps my body start on a real path; I am now in the process of movement, and that first step stirs more movement. In this way, it's part of the landing process, but it's a landing that has a five-mile radius.

When we started designing our house, we had a lot of specific visions. We wanted multiple buildings connected by glass. We imagined a low-lying feel. We wanted hardworking materials and substantial pieces so we wouldn't have to worry too much about chipping edges or things getting blown away. But we also realized we couldn't have it all or have everything exactly the way we'd imagined; we had to remind ourselves again and again to hold it more lightly. We took others' counsel and changed room sizes. We crossed out some stonework. We modified to suit what others could actually accomplish instead of pushing them too far past their skill set. And we tried to let ourselves be taught too, because it was our first time and we had a million things to learn. It's like driving forward with one hand on the steering wheel and the other reaching out the window in the wind.

That's how I want to create and create with others: one hand on the wheel, one in the wind.

Good things to remember:
You don't have to do it brilliantly the first time.
You can be a haven to work with and create alongside.
You might mess up.
You might need to get really humble.

In the end, there will come a time when you have to stop revising. You can't revise forever or keep killing darlings. You need to make your final choices and put down the last period. Hit send. Put the stake in the ground.

And if you've given it space to breathe along the way, you'll be ready.

Create Little Scenes

I OFTEN START BY MAKING A LITTLE SCENE.

One thing that will shut down hospitality or creative living or new dreams is when I get too overwhelmed by the thing I want to do, and all I see are the potential outages, flaws, or chaos that seems like it could never go away—and so I stop before I start. This is when I try making small scenes. I forget the big finale for a minute and start with one section. One corner. One table.

When I used to draw more, I was very into realism and detail. I wanted a portrait that felt like it was *alive*. But I couldn't even get close. My proportions were off, the features too cliché, the movement and nuance not there at all.

So my mom, who had been an art teacher, taught me the grid system. You lightly pencil a grid over the photograph or whatever you want to recreate, then go square by square instead of all at once. You force yourself to do only one small piece at a time, and you don't even touch the rest. It's how you eat an elephant.

When my friends and I created the camping event for women, we had to do a whole lot of making little scenes. We couldn't transform the five hundred acres of Ohio fields and woods into a campsite wonderland. We had to forget full transformation and just dot the area with lovely things. We put string lights in a section of the wrecked barn. We set up pretty signs in front of the piecemeal farm equipment. And since we couldn't find an affordable way to cover up the audacious row of bright blue portable toilets, we made the insides pleasant instead: tea lights, a glass jar with lavender, messages taped in gold to the inside of the door.

We couldn't do it all, but we could do some.

When you're looking at something large (even if it's your life as a whole) and you want to adjust something significant, it's easy to fall into the trap of believing it's too much to tackle. But if you zero in on one or two things, like brightening up one corner of a messy room or choosing one night of the year to create a candlelit dinner and invite your friends—this is still movement. And often, by making a few little scenes, it's easier to create the next few little scenes. Just like starting a draft helps you finish the next version. Before you know it, you might have even eaten the whole elephant.

So pencil-sketch a grid over the thing you want to do.

Choose one square to focus on.

Begin.

Make Kits

I once stumbled upon an idea that I've never let go of, because it's amazingly helpful in this world of creating scenes, setting up events, being a caretaker. It's all about kits.

KIT:
A PORTABLE
COLLECTION OF
SUPPLIES FOR
CREATING AN
EXPERIENCE

I found the idea in one of my mom's old etiquette books. The advice was to have a tray, napkins, and drink supplies ready so when a guest drops by, you already have something prepared that's easy to pull out. Then you simply add drinks and ice. When the host tray is ready ahead of time, it's easier to invite someone inside (and you're more likely to do it) since you're not scurrying around making an impromptu plan or feeling like you have nothing to offer.

I've since taken that idea and applied it in other ways. Now I make kits for creating events, for hospitality setups, for day trips, for bringing visitors to the house. I mostly use plastic laundry baskets and trays to hold the items, or sometimes a sturdy canvas bag. I like containers that are open so you can easily see what's inside. And I always go for containers with good handles, because I'm often carrying kits a good distance, hauling them in and out of my van, and setting them on the ground during setup.

Here are some of my go-to kits:

OUTDOOR COFFEE DELIVERY KIT

high-edged tray
*coffee cups**
jar for cream
sugar bowl

spoon
kitchen towel (to line the tray
   and catch drips)

** I use ceramic cups if someone is sticking around
and a paper cup with a lid for someone who needs
the freedom to hit the road and take it with them.*

VAN HANGOUT KIT

candle and matches
big pillow
blanket

a few books
bottled drinks

SMALL OUTDOOR DINNER KIT

laundry basket
pretty sheets for table covering
cloth napkins
stack of ceramic plates
glass cups wrapped in cloth
   napkins

silverware sets
sharp knife wrapped in a
   dishcloth
wine bottle opener
menu items

WATCHING-A-GAME KIT

*snacks in plasticware for easy
  passing around
drawing pad and pens for extra
  entertainment*

*towel for wet bleachers and spills
cash for concessions*

OVERNIGHT GUEST KIT

See "How to: Make a Guest
Space" in part 1.

OTHER KITS

Think of times you find yourself scrambling to collect what
you need for certain occasions,
especially the ones that come
up on short notice or the ones
you want to dream about ahead
of time and add items to slowly.
Make a list of kits that would
be helpful to have on hand and
what would go inside them.
Write them here.

_____

_____

_____

_____

_____

_____

_____

_____

_____

_____

Put It All on the Table

IN THE DESIGN PROCESS, it does wonders to make a physical mood board. When I was overwhelmed by house-building and design choices, I realized maybe I was struggling because I had only made word lists and digital mock-ups. What I actually needed was to go back to my windowsill-collection days. Make the process physical. Make it real-world, in front of me, like an architect building a small-scale model of what's to come.

So I cleared off our biggest table and started adding every tile sample, every paint selection, every grout strip, every piece of countertop stone that we were considering or had already chosen. I needed all these things in front of me, in the same space, so I could see what was working—and what wasn't.

Ryan and I immediately found things that didn't work as a whole. We changed colors, built more continuity, and decided we wanted some surprises like a pink sink to break up all the earth tones around it. I don't think we would have figured these things out with words or screens alone.

When you're putting it all on the table, I think it's also important to add existing life pieces or things that represent the way you live, because those elements will also share the space.

For us, it's little things:

a stack of novels,
a few of our chipped dishes and cups,
a scribbled note,
my grandfather's photograph,
a tarnished bottle opener,
my dad's leather duffel,
our kids' handmade ceramics,
sheets of white paper,
sheets of homework,
art with bent edges, and
fruit.

These things—representing the people who live in our house and the way we live—are really the main characters, the most wonderful parts. The tile and carpet samples and other material selections are fresh additions. But if those additions become too much the main focus when you're "putting it on the table," it's going to feel stale or empty or not really *you* in the end. The point of combining and layering is to tell a fuller, more realistic, more natural story.

But there's something else too—something harder to put into words. I think it goes back to the idea of landing and being comfortable in the fullness of who we are as humans. I don't want to compartmentalize or aim for perfection. I know that new tile floors will get marred by dirty feet, soap scum, bad moods, broken eggs.

I don't want to move into a new house or a remodeled room or something else that I've designed or created, and feel like I'm stepping into a display instead of home. I don't want to make a photo shoot, as tempting as it is to try and pull that off. Because then I'll wonder how to hold and carry myself inside it. I'll wonder if I'll break something. I'll wonder how to brush my teeth in a sink like that or comb my daughter's hair over a floor like this or slide to the ground after a mess of a day in a hallway that didn't know it was going to have to support me.

I believe we need homes that let us sink into them with our whole bodies and lives. And so we should build and shape them that way from the outset. Because messes of days will happen, right among the wonder and joy. There will be mistakes and low moods and broken cabinets that live side by side with great love and beautiful sounds and bread baking in the kitchen.

PUTTING IT ON THE TABLE: COLLECTING MATERIALS, FABRICS, COLORS, AND OBJECTS, THEN SETTING THEM ALL TOGETHER AS A LOOK INTO WHAT YOU'LL BE CREATING

Feed Five Hundred

Women in the Woods

Gather twenty friends who love to get dirty, haul tables through grass, design on the fly, and cook over an open fire.

Tell these twenty friends that this whole thing is audacious and some things will fall apart, but as long as we get bread and butter on the table, we'll call it a win.

Sell very cheap tickets to five hundred women so everyone is able to join. Give away tickets to those who need them.

Use that money creatively: borrow chairs from a church and metal fire rings from park rangers; buy rolls of white paper for tablecloths; get discounts by casting a vision to local businesses that have extras.

Have a second meeting with your twenty friends and invite a woman who knows how to cook for film crews and large crowds. Give her your budget. Watch her reimagine her first plan. Clap when she says she has a new idea . . . "If those five hundred women can help us make the food . . . this could work."

Ask your baker friend to come up with a dessert that can be cooked in a cast-iron pot, and when she tells you it's going to be a cake with fresh blackberry compote, hail her as a champion.

Buy everything in bulk; pay attention to sales. Ask others to pay attention to sales for you, because it's time to start giving away responsibilities.

Buy gold paint, pale paint, navy paint.

Get cheap fabric, and tear it into a million strips. Make ribbon garlands to hang over the tables, and have women write prayers on them.

Rent string lights and pay to have them hung under the rented white tent, because it's so high up and you can't add another thing to the team's to-do list.

You can also do this for ten women and scale it way back. Or for five thousand. But if it's five thousand, you might want to invite Jesus.

| BREAKING GROUND

Learn to cook a chicken over a flame. Taste test. Try again.

Build a big cement-block stove to cook half the chickens all at once.

Buy a ton of foil.

*Ask the five hundred women attending the event to bring a white
plate, silverware, and a wine glass. When some ask if they can bring
plastic, be brave and insist: glass will sparkle.*

*Buy boxes and boxes of twist-off-cap wine, and ask boldly for a
discount. Remind the wine people it's basically free marketing to five
hundred women who are going to want to remember this night.*

*Create a play-by-play checklist for every minute of the meal prep, every
phase of the cooking, and every last minute of setup. You won't have
a megaphone; you can't be everywhere at once.*

*Get to the land early. A few days, if possible. Start receiving all the
rentals, all the truck deliveries.*

*Set up stations for the next day: butter, salad, chicken, fish, carrots,
cake, compote.*

*On the day of the event, welcome the women into camp. Sing. Run to
meet them at the road. Make up a dance. Be ridiculous so all the
strangers feel more at ease.*

*After everyone has set up their tents and had long stretches of play
and solitude and tried their hand at chopping firewood, invite your
guests into the massive cooking experiment.*

Cheer them on.

Put out fires.

Bring drinks to your leaders. Fill their pockets with belief.

Laugh it off when chickens burn and batter spills.

*When things take way, way longer than your checklist had in mind,
hand out predinner wine.*

Believe in communion.

Invite everyone to the hand-painted, garland-strewn, candlelit tables.

See their faces light up because of what we all just accomplished.

Finally, feast.

**AN EXPERIENCE I WANT TO
CREATE FOR OTHERS**

_____

_____

_____

_____

_____

_____

_____

_____

_____

RECIPE:

Honey Butter in Jars*

FOR FIVE WOMEN

01 Put 4 sticks (1 pound) of room-temperature unsalted butter in a mixing bowl.

02 Using a spoon or spatula, whip the butter until it's light and fluffy.

03 Add ¼ cup of honey.

04 Add 1 teaspoon of salt.

05 Remove leaves from 8 sprigs of flat-leaf parsley and 8 sprigs of basil. Chop into small pieces over the butter.

06 Mix it in.

07 Distribute butter into 5 little jars with lids.

FOR FIVE HUNDRED WOMEN

01 Put 400 sticks (100 pounds) of room-temperature unsalted butter into huge mixing bowls.

02 Using spoons or spatulas and a whole lot of friends, whip the butter until it's light and fluffy.

03 Add 25 cups of honey.

04 Add 100 teaspoons (2-ish cups) of salt.

05 Gather a bunch of volunteers and remove leaves from 800 sprigs of flat-leaf parsley and 800 sprigs of basil. Don't really count out 800; just guess. Chop into small pieces over the butter.

06 Mix it in.

07 Distribute butter into 500 little jars with lids.

* Recipe contributed by Beth Thomas.

In the Middle of It

"THIS ISN'T WORKING!" she shout-whispered at me, as we stood behind the five hundred women who had come to the camping event we had just birthed and released.

The women were all gathered in the barn, and the lull in our sequence of events was real. It was a lull that had turned to some discomfort for those of us leading. The promised food wasn't even close to being ready. The live music from the stage was wobbling and losing its edge. There was some murmuring, some glancing around. I saw one of our leaders bent over in tears.

That moment is when I wanted to on-the-spot quit. I wanted to quit because one of our leaders was bent over and another leader had shout-whispered and I felt such embarrassment and fury that I just sank. I began convincing myself there was no way, *no way*, any of it was going to work. I went from having all the energy in the world to believing I had messed everything up, so I might as well fly solo for the rest of my life. All from one shout-whisper that it wasn't working from a woman I loved and who loved me.

"Then try to *fix it*," I shout-whispered back. She pushed off the wall we were both leaning against and hurried away.

Sometimes I'd rather just tell the beautiful bits and skate over the drop zones and pitfalls. But of course I can't—and shouldn't. When you're making and building new things (even if they're small), you will usually face something at some point that makes you want to quit. You'll want to throw away whatever it is you're working on, say mean things to yourself or the people around you, hang your head.

It's that part of creating when you hit the "quit now before you think you'll die" wall. For some, it happens before they even start or pull the trigger. For others, it's the middle. For others, it's when you're only about 10 percent from the finish line and you figure you'd better call it a day because somehow you know you won't "win." That's how upending it can be to make something. (Read *The War of Art* by Steven Pressfield for more about overcoming resistance. It's phenomenal.)

My friend came back and found me slumped against the wall.

"Let's just give them the wine early." She smiled, and I jumped up to hug her.

When you're making something, hold steady—and don't quit because your guests are glancing around wondering what's next. People can wait. Don't quit because someone is struggling or shout-whispering. Don't quit because you're afraid. Instead, let yourself explore options or face fears and discuss new solutions if needed. Adjust, but don't shut down. Give grace and take a deep breath. Bear-hug your cocreators and remember why you started in the first place.

Besides, the women *loved* the early wine.

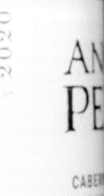

Giving People Their Safe

WE CONVINCED OUR FRIEND LaTasha to do Woman Camp with us. She's wise and hilarious to have around, and people want to follow her. It took some arm twisting, though, because she's a regular-showers and sleep-in-a-bed kind of human. But because she wanted to serve other women, she agreed.

The first night at camp, she told me later, she felt so out of place. She didn't like being outside and exhausted and smelly, and in the thick of so many people all day when she's an introvert at heart. So at the campfire, she told us she was going to bed early and left before we could convince her to stay. She thought her tent would feel like a respite, but it didn't. She said she lay on her cot for hours waiting for sleep to come, with voices in her head saying, *You're not cut out for this. You definitely don't belong here.*

When I went to camp as a kid, Sibyl came to my cabin and tucked me in. Out of the hundreds of campers, I don't know how many of us she visited, but I imagine it was a lot of us. And I would immediately feel better after she visited, after her one quick gesture that settled my spirit. I think whenever you bring someone into a new place—even if it's a wonderful guest spot you've set up in your home or a good meal at a table—it's good to keep reminding people they are wanted, they belong.

I had the thought that night to do the same for LaTasha, because big memories stick.

As I starting walking toward her tent, I felt a bit foolish. As adults, we don't usually tuck other adults into bed. But I went over to her zippered-shut door, pretended to knock, and crawled in. She laughed when she saw me, but I could also see her discomfort. I had been there too. So I fixed her sleeping bag arrangement like Ryan had shown me to do, kissed her on the forehead, said, "Good night, you angel," and crawled back out.

Sibyl has been my safe. I had a chance to be LaTasha's safe. And LaTasha has been Kinesha's safe, Andrea's safe, Jennie's safe. Because this is how it happens. We learn to repeat the meaningful things that are done for us, and we start to see more ways to do it. And more often than not, they are so simple to do.

You see someone stuck or awkwardly waiting around or struggling to figure something out, so you join them. You ask them to help you so they have something to focus on. You do something ridiculous to make them laugh. You give them extra firewood and tell them it's because they're the most deserving person in the world. You give them your jacket or take out their trash or deliver a handful of flowers. You give them a cart. You stay with them until they seem ready to be on their own again.

Elbow Grease

SOMETIMES YOU STUMBLE into a new way of taking care of others that feels outside the plan.

As we were running the camps for women, we had to throw our whole bodies into them. We didn't have money to hire extra help; we were the extras. So we loaded trailers, built grills, moved water tanks and hay bales and stages. Sometimes we complained, but we said it was good for us, and we said our guests were worth it.

But we noticed as we were doing all this labor that many of the women we were serving or creating the experience for—they wanted to work with us too. They might have been worn out from taking care of toddlers or running around their offices and houses, but the appeal of new physical labor or running big machinery or riding around in the back of a pickup truck to deliver supplies must have looked exciting—maybe even freeing. It also opened the door to letting others be creators too.

So we handed out new jobs and tractor keys. We brought in a hundred axes and said, "We need your strength." We fueled up industrial log splitters. We made group dumpster runs and hustled around like wild women, dripping with sweat and trash.

We had some injuries. We made mistakes and broke things that were hard to fix. But somehow it turned out okay, after a few apologies and mends. And after nights like these, we sank into our plates at dinner, happy-exhausted, already telling stories about what we'd learned to do. It made breaking bread and time around the table that much sweeter.

I keep this trick in my back pocket now. When I host a dinner party, I don't do all the work ahead of time so that everyone can make a contribution, have something to put a hand to, have a purpose, even if it's small. And of course, it's a massive help. Because we all need extra hands and small contributions, even if we're the ones who made the invite.

Work Up a Good Sweat

Sling around some firewood.

Learn to use a piece of machinery you've never used.

Mow the grass.

*Ask to join someone else who's doing something
    you've never done.*

Build a fire.

Cook over it.

Stand on a ladder.

Use a pressure washer.

Turn a rock pile into a path.

Move things by hand.

Drive stick shift. (I still can't.)

Lift weights so you're ready.

Sprint down a road.

Howl and sweat.

Sleep.

Bowls and Chairs and Pockets

WHEN RYAN WAS AWAY for military training or deployments and I was home alone in our Italian rental, I started eating all my meals out of bowls but didn't realize until I was a week's worth of bowls into the habit. I looked into the sink one night, and there was the proof. Dinner had been pasta, oatmeal, olives.

I would carry the bowls out to the porch, sit on the warm terra-cotta floor, and eat from my lap. A plate would have been precarious. A bowl was just right.

Bowls are like good chairs: they are good for holding. Good chairs let you pull your knees in, drape your legs over the soft sides, sink deep against the upholstered back to read or daydream or talk to your neighbor. If I were only allowed one piece of furniture in my life, I'd choose a good chair.

When I'm designing or putting out items for guests, I think:

HOW CAN THIS SURROUND SOMEONE?

WHERE WOULD A PERSON GO, INSIDE THIS DESIGN, IF THEY NEEDED TO BE HELD?

WHERE ARE THE PLACES THAT FEEL LIKE POCKETS?

Bowls and chairs are like apron pockets, hugs, a grouping of feather pillows, the bucket seats of a car. They hold you.

Garages Work Too

SHE CAME IN FROM TEXAS, Charis did, after we made a little spot for her to sleep in our son's room—pulling out the slingshots and worn quilts and adding a pink water glass, a few chosen books, a white coverlet.

Charis's plane landed, and I found her by the sliding glass doors, already laughing, at the baggage claim. That night we went for pasta and a long walk in long sweaters. One conversation led to the next and to the next, as it does when you eat pasta and walk and drive around after flying across the country and the day still has room in it.

At the end of the night, I pulled into the garage and turned off the van. Charis was mid-sentence, so we stayed there without opening the doors so she could finish. But her sentence didn't finish; it kept going, because sometimes it takes time to get to the thing at the heart of the thing. A few minutes turned into a few hours, there on the vinyl van seats, the leftover pasta still boxed between us.

Charis told me this later:

> *We sat in the van after pulling into the garage. There was no one who would walk in suddenly without notice, no chance of someone overhearing or catching me off guard as I was baring my heart.*
>
> *Everyone was asleep inside. It was late, so there was nothing else to do. That space was set apart and safe, still and dark. Like a bunker, you know? Compact and protected and strong. That's how it felt.*
>
> *And there was something about the sacredness of that small space and not feeling even the slightest rush or push that let my stories come out—stories I had not yet told a friend.*
>
> *We sat there amid the tenderness of the deep experiences I shared—the shame and pain and desperate hope all balled up together. It was a rare thing; we were in a territory I hadn't gone to before.*
>
> *I felt nearly gutted as I just let it all spill out, without worrying how I would clean it up or what that would look like. And it happened in a concrete garage in suburbia, with cat bowls and grease stains. Yet it was a place of healing. I felt free to take the space and knew it was open for me.*

Sometimes we just need garages.

Let People Wander

I LOVE A GOOD RUSH, a dynamic itinerary, a fast-paced walk with purpose. But I'm learning this rarely feels like the gait for hospitality. For adventure, yes. For high productivity and the enthused making of things, for sure.

But letting people wander and wandering alongside or nearby them—this, I have learned, is a gift of a thing to build into hospitality. It's often overlooked or pushed out of the way because we think if we're hosting someone, we need to be full-on entertaining. So we end up packing experiences tight. We don't want a dull or quiet moment; we don't want our guests to be restless, distracted. We don't want to be a failed host.

But I have begun to trust that guests will be okay with a little space to turn around in. And I need the space too. I can't be hospitable for long if I try to fill every crack and crevice.

Once I had a teacher stay overnight at our house. She was tired and too far from home to make a late-night drive. When she arrived, we talked for a few minutes and I could tell she was tired, and instead of trying to build momentum or work extra hard to be an engaging host, I tried something I hadn't before: "Do you want to call it a night?" The relief on her face was clear. Rest and solitude can be a wild gift of a thing when you're short on it.

In the morning, she left after coffee and bread. It was plain and simple. I held back from asking questions. I didn't make suggestions or create detours or a fancy breakfast. Her rest wasn't about me, so I didn't need to direct it. And honestly, I was busy. I didn't have time to make a fancy breakfast.

Simplicity and space to recover are often the abundance people are looking for. It's like leaving white space in the design of a book: you give people room to take a breath before going toward the next thing.

Gravel, Because It Sounds Beautiful

MY SISTERS AND I USED TO HELP my mom clean a blind woman's house. The woman liked to hear the kitchen faucet running into her metal sink and the twisting sound the faucet made when she turned it off. "It's how I hear my home," she told me.

I think that's one of the most beautiful things I've ever heard.

How do you hear your home?

We're bringing in gravel for the new driveway, and that will be part of our sound. We will hear car tires rolling over it, feet crunching across it, suitcase wheels bumping along it. These sounds will begin to mark our home, let us hear where we are, help anchor us to what we share.

Think of the sounds that create your home, your haven. Maybe it's the opening of an oven, loud laughter, extra "good night" calls from the bottom of the stairs. Maybe it's low music after dinner. Book pages turning in bed. Water running in a bathtub. People knocking on the front door.

HOW DO YOU HEAR
YOUR HOME? WHAT
SOUNDS DO YOU WANT
TO HEAR MORE OF?

SOMETIMES IT'S EASIER
TO HEAR THEM IF WE
CLOSE OUR EYES.

Place Mats

I HADN'T USED PLACE MATS in what felt like forever.

Ryan and I were both working full-time, we had some combination of babies and toddlers, and I remember staring at our table late one night and falling apart. Everything felt stained, plain, and dull. I didn't mind the mac and cheese or hot dogs or basically just repeating lunch food at dinner. But what I longed for were moments of beauty. I hadn't stopped to create them in one of our most high-traffic spaces and a place I wanted to love.

And so I said enough is enough: I started using place mats. Under the hot dogs and mac and cheese. It helped. It was both real and symbolic, and I needed that elevation in the midst of those days.

When you're in the deep throes of life, maybe all you need is a stack of place mats to lift your heart. Or maybe it's not place mats, but something else that will remind you that you are still a creator, still have the time for beauty, still can make small changes to elevate a plain day.

I would apologize for making a trivial statement about place mats being like little miracles, except that I'm putting them on our table tonight, and I know what will happen.

Aperol Spritz and Wood Chips

It's a gorgeous drink, but I should start by saying this: I will take a bite out of an orange without even peeling it. So a bitter, citrusy, bubbling drink is spot on in my book. However, this easy cocktail—which is probably the very first drink we had in Italy—is not *quite* like biting an unpeeled orange. It's like a tiny bite. Mixed with bubbles and a dash of sugar.

½ Aperol liquor

½ Prosecco or a favorite, non-alcoholic champagne

Poured over a glass of ice

Make a couple glassfuls and set them on a tray. Take them out to the woodpile where you're burning things with your sister and just live in that perfect combination of ash and grove.

PART 3 | *coming* HOME

Runaway Bunnies

IT WAS A SMALL BOOK I often chose at bedtime: *The Runaway Bunny*. My mom would read it to me, and I think she must have loved it too, because of how she smiled when I asked for it.

It's the story of a mother rabbit who keeps telling her little bunny how she will find him, no matter where he goes. If he becomes a rock on a mountain, she says she will become a mountain climber and climb all the way to where he is. If he turns himself into a sailboat, she will turn herself into the wind and find him on the waves. If he becomes a bird and flies far away, she will become the tree he comes home to.

The mother promises to keep finding her child, no matter who he attempts to become or what places he tries to inhabit and how long it takes him to land.

Finally, in the end, he decides he'll stay next to her after all. She gives him dinner, and the last illustration is the two of them inside their rabbit home—in a glowing, gold circle under the shelter of a tree.

"You'll never want to come home," my uncle said to me.

I was nineteen and had asked my parents if they would sit down with me so I could explain: I wanted a break from college. I wanted to move across the country to California, where my grandmother used to live, perched as she had been perched on the side of a mountain, nestled in the junipers and laurels and morning sunrise.

I dreamed about the summer my family had spent in California, my sister and me sitting on the cantilevered porch, eating cherries, spitting the pits high in the air, and laughing our heads off. Early in the mornings, we walked the steep roads alongside the house, picked wild succulents and flowers to make perfume in my grandmother's empty bottles. I remember the heavy fog of the mornings, the barley soup I ate in town, the endless rows of artichoke fields.

I wanted to go back.

My uncle overheard me from our kitchen and stuck his head around the corner.

"Liz, you'll fall in love with it there," he added, moving to stand next to my parents, now at full attention. He was the uncle who handed me old novels about roaming the world and pieces of Bible verses scratched across birthday cards—"May his face shine upon you"—year after year. He was a journeyman, a believer in second and twentieth chances. He was gruff and incredibly loud, but he knew the way to hearts.

"I promise I'll come back home," I said to all three of them through my tears. I'd always carried some dread about leaving home, even if it was only for the day. And it was hard to ask for permission to leave again after I had been floundering that year and wasn't really proving that I would do well even farther away.

I had started my first year of college and made it two-thirds of the way through before I tanked. I was confused and at odds with myself. The whole idea of college and sororities and parties felt like a show, a dulling performance that I didn't have the energy or wherewithal to sustain.

"I was thinking I could live in the valley by the general store," I continued. "I'll get a job. Then I'll go back to college next year," I finished, trailing off.

"Okay," my parents both said together, nodding. And it became one of those wondrous moments in my life when I felt the immense gift of being released freely, trusted abundantly. They were letting me go without raised eyebrows, without conditions, without a return ticket home.

I didn't dread leaving that time, maybe because my parents' release came so freely, maybe because it was simply the right thing at the right time—as unexpected as it was. I packed my bags and got on a plane. My sister went with me to help get me settled because she is so wonderful at that. We found a bedroom for rent in an old woman's house in the mountains where my grandmother used to live—near the general store, just as I'd hoped. I found a job serving expensive coffee and breakfast pastries in town. My aunt, who I didn't know well yet, who also lived in that town and didn't have children of her own, invited my sister and me over for dinner. After we ate, we stood on her driveway, and she pointed to a tiny old car in the yard covered with a tarp.

"It should work pretty well! You can use it while you live out here." She smiled.

And she was right: it only pretty-well worked, so I drove it when it did, then biked or walked for miles when it didn't.

I got a library card and hauled plastic-covered books to my new bedroom, filled the shared fridge with apples and cream and day-old pastries from the coffee shop. I worked early in the fog-dark mornings, handing out bitter espresso drinks to construction workers and rich hippies, then scrubbed marble tables when the café emptied and only the newspaper readers were left, and the retired illustrator who would sometimes leave a scrap of his work under a coffee cup.

I kept paper and pens in my apron, and I wrote on the back steps when I had a free minute, or just sat quietly with the old roses growing between rocks, petting dogs that walked by, saying hi to the other shopkeepers and the town gardeners, beginning to learn about their lives too.

I was trying out landings.

I was becoming a rock. A sailboat. A bird.

Then one night after work, after a half of a year of life in the mountain laurels and coffee shop, I carried my dinner in a plastic bag to the ocean. At the dunes, some kids were pulling out pieces of driftwood and hauling them back to a group of parents who were gathered by a cooler, assembling paper-plate dinners and holding babies. One of the dads helped the kids turn their pile of debris into a fort, and then they sat under it with their meals on plates, laughing and flinging sand and crying when it got in their eyes, chasing birds when they finished. A toddler fell asleep in her chair.

And suddenly I knew it was time to go home. I was finished and ready to return, ready to be back in the gold glowing circle under the shelter of a tree eating dinner with the people I loved.

I hugged my aunt who had taken care of me so well, who had read my story drafts while I read her essays, who had walked with me during the days along the shore and helped me see who I was just a little bit better, a little bit better.

Together we draped the tarp back over her little car and I told her I'd be back one day and I'd treasure us always. I returned my library books, hugged my coworkers goodbye, and set the last of the apples outside the back door for the feral cats and raccoons.

I got home in time for Christmas. I stood next to my three sisters in the kitchen as we peeled persimmons for a salad and baked pecan pies while my dad built a fire.

"I have someone I think you should meet," one of my sisters said. "Do you remember Ryan?"

I smiled. I did.

I flew back to California last week. Twenty-five years after my life there, twenty-three years after marrying the one who makes me smile.

As soon as I got off the plane and drove past the artichoke fields that led to the Pacific, I felt it happen: the coming-togetherness. A feeling of a deep internal mending like a quiet homecoming of who I was before and who I had become. The long passages and layers of time. All the years of trying, stretching, landing.

backyard forts
runaway bunnies
the forgotten blade of grass
burying a necklace
the blind woman's faucet
abruptly leaving college
braving California
searching, collecting, attempting
finding Ryan
finding Italy
a piece of chocolate on September 11
art school revelations
military separations
the power of worship
the power of healing
babies
landing
expanding
homecoming
here
now

I pulled over on the side of the California road with my eyes on the high waves of the Pacific and the surfers who wouldn't give up. I smiled because I wasn't lonely anymore. I smiled because I had found places to land and people to take care of and people who take care of me too. I smiled because I was learning to look at all of it—not just the beautiful and wondrous parts, but the broken and off-kilter pieces too.

I rolled down the windows and closed my eyes. It felt so good to be still.

**RELATIONSHIPS I WANT
TO CONNECT WITH MORE
DEEPLY**

_____

_____

_____

_____

_____

_____

_____

_____

_____

_____

To Build a House

WE'RE CLOSE TO FINISHING THE HOUSE.
The walls are up, the windows in. It's a wild winter in the Midwest and not a good time at all to be moving or filling box trucks with furniture. It's a terrible time to pour concrete or create a driveway. But sometimes this is how it goes.

Ryan and I trudge through deep snow to get to the moving truck, and it's so cold we don't even talk for fear that we'll snap. Some of our family and nieces and nephews come to help, and they brighten everything immensely. Our friends bring carryout, and we eat deli sandwiches daily. It is almost Christmas, and that's when we move in: the night before. We will skip pecan pies and pomegranates this year.

We put up a small tree (a fake one), and my sweet nieces hang ornaments with our kids. A few shatter, and a few roll across the bare floors with nothing to stop them. Ryan's aunt brings groceries and dish towels. I search for the wrapped gifts in the back of the box truck, and we set them out on the new floor and try to imagine how one day this place will feel like home. It doesn't yet, because it's only just begun to hold us, but we trust it will.

We tuck the kids into bed and then Ryan and I stay up late into the night, unpacking more boxes to get out the coffee maker, the candles. The wind is powerful and fierce: we watch huge old trees behind our house sway, groan under ice. I feel the fear creeping in: what if this house falls, what if it's all too much, what if it doesn't work and it never quite feels like home? But I make myself assess the fear instead of just letting it build. I try to understand what's reasonable, what isn't. What we can control and what we can't.

And I remind myself that this is what I often come against when a big moment is happening or about to: I start to imagine failure. It's a pattern, whether it's a house, a camp, a book, a landing. But seeing the pattern I follow is like clearing the storm. I am not a stranger to myself anymore.

I fall asleep.

The morning is quiet and vast, even in the span of a few minutes. Limbs have fallen from trees and lie across the hills around us, around our faraway neighbors, but the house is standing strong. Our kids are one by one coming to sit on the steps, same as they've always done, even though now they're tall and gangly. I rush at them, pulling their warm, sleepy bodies against mine in an awkward heap and loving them beyond every measure. Ryan joins the heap of us, then the day unrolls into parents' homes, others' laughter, others' arms. And once again the reminder is there like a bright star: it's not the place; it's the people.

"Was it worth it?" a delivery man asks us.

Many people ask the same question when they pull into the gravel driveway. Maybe because building a house is such a huge undertaking and investment. But I also think people ask and wonder because we're so often looking out and around to see what is meaningful and worth it in life. We look to one another as barometers, sounding boards, possible pathways. We wonder if we should try on the same shoes.

Friends and family have seen our delight in building this house, putting all the pieces and visions together, making something come to life that started as a windowsill collection and scraps of paper. They've also seen the walls we've hit, the choices that shook us, the pain we felt leaving the neighborhood of my two sisters.

I don't know how to answer the delivery guy, not in a concise way. Because nothing about this process has been concise. I think that's how it is when you make or take part in something significant, whether it's a house you'll live in, a business you'll open, a movement you'll get off the ground.

But in the rise and fall of this process, we've always known it isn't *really* about a house. The house is beautiful, and we are deeply thankful. It's shareable, spacious, set apart. But it's also a huge responsibility, and much to manage. This won't be easy, even if it's a dream come true. Things will break; trees will fall; task lists will often be longer than the time we have to give them.

Ryan tells the delivery guy it's been good; it's been worth it for our family. But then I hear him say—and thank God this is the kind of man I married— "But we all have different worthwhiles."

Then I watch him begin walking around our half-frozen property, picking up dropped nails and empty cans from the workers—always on the lookout for things that are out of place and need to be taken care of. I can still picture him getting off an airplane when we were dating, wearing his starched military uniform, walking toward me with his duffel bags and dreams, committed and steady.

Yes.

Ryan is worth it.

Our children are worth it.

Our family, our friends are worth it.

The people we meet and the ones who roll down the gravel drive of this new rambling house: they are worth it too.

We all are.

I am.

You are.

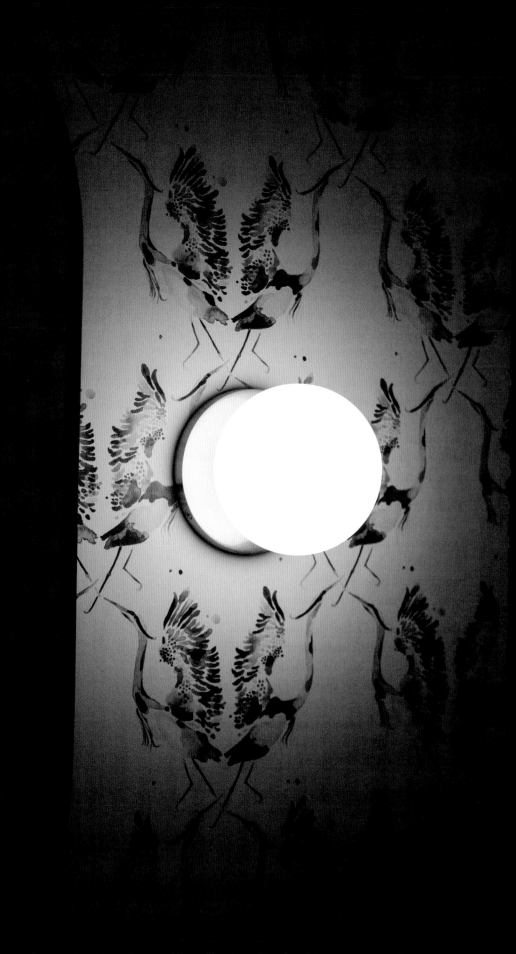

Epsom Salts at the Gas Station

WE STOOD ON OPPOSITE SIDES of the gas station aisle. I was looking at cheap wine; she was looking at the body-care products. Her phone rang, but I noticed she didn't answer it.

"I bet we're both looking for the same thing," she said without looking up, and I laughed. She held up what she found: a bag of Epsom salts.

"Post-workout soak?" I asked. I had seen other runners stretching their legs outside the gas station and she looked like an athlete, too.

"Nope. Just recovering from taking care of other people."

I nodded.

"It's my day off though, so I'm taking care of myself."

She said goodbye and took her bag of salts to the register. I picked up a bag too and followed in her wake.

Sometimes gas stations have just what you need.

Sometimes you need to go somewhere else. To the water. To the hills. To a place where people are singing with their eyes closed.

Maybe you need to return to a place you once lived. Or a field without fence or phone.

Maybe you need a good counselor. A true friend. A place at the table.

For years I cared so deeply about creating havens for others that I didn't realize how much it mattered to create them for myself. I don't mean I was selfless or uncared for—I had plenty of needs met

and good things happening, and I was treasured by the ones who matter most. But I often didn't spend the time to figure out where I felt safe or not safe, where I was too weary to give but gave anyway, how to close a door and just say, "I'm finished for now," "I can't meet today," "I can't do that for you."

And when you don't live honestly like this, the fallout can be significant. You eventually run out of steam or hit an unhealthy wall or turn resentful. And you usually end up believing you're the full solution to whatever is needed while you try to carry it all when it wasn't all yours to carry.

A few years ago, I went in for an MRI. I was losing my balance, getting my left and right mixed up, missing the bottom step on my way down the stairs. One day I fell so hard after missing a step that what I normally would have laughed off didn't feel funny anymore. I lay there crying, and Ryan ran in from another room.

The MRI came back clear. The doctor called me to go over it and once again asked me about the stress in my life. I said it was definitely under control. Yes, I was working hard in a leadership role, and yes, we had three young children who I wanted to be fully present with and a lot of family and relationships and expectations and responsibilities to uphold. Yes, yes, yes. *Don't we all?* I thought. *How could I complain? I love what I do, and I love my life, so really it's all definitely okay.*

But in the back of my mind, I thought about the times I would panic. How I'd sit in my car for an extra minute to will it all back together. Tell myself to be stronger, or manage time better, or just find a new solution to holding everything I was holding, because I always believed there was a way to figure it out without letting anything go. And I remembered being in my tent at Woman Camp, in the middle of the night, my mind fraught with fear as I imagined all the ways I needed to lead and protect and just couldn't. I had visions of rampant fires, wolves, stranger attacks. Fear is an unreasonable beast, and I was tipping.

When Ryan's vision went haywire, he was driving a big camp van down the highway. He was on his way to visit a college campus, share about the power of a camp ministry and what it was doing for all of us.

His vision started flipping like an old TV station with a broken channel, black and white. He inched his way off the highway. His friends picked him up, and I met them in the ER. It was déjà vu: the doctor asked if he had been under stress. Ryan said that his work was hard, yes, and yes, yes, yes. The doctor nodded; I wondered how many of us he'd seen like this.

"We'll do an MRI just to be sure," he said, and I put my head in my hands. "But I think it's going to come back clear. I think there's something else you need to change."

People told us this could happen. We were warned and encouraged to pay attention, to not ignore what our bodies were telling us. But sometimes your body beats you to the punch. It starts to shut down and throw flags until you're forced to make a change.

Ryan quit his job. Eventually, I did too. We started quieter, simpler jobs. Ryan felt his peace return;

I stopped losing my balance. But we also learned that it isn't necessarily the job that is spinning you haywire on the inside: it's how you're doing the job and what you've accepted. It's when you don't tell people when you need help or when expectations are impossibly high. It's when you have nightmares but don't work through them. It's when you duck away from taking care of yourself or setting calm boundaries because you're so bent on the needs piling up around you and how you'll solve them all.

There will always be needs piled up around you. Something will always be broken. Someone will always be asking for help or demanding too much. But you aren't the only one out there. Even if it feels like you are—you aren't.

If you're losing your balance or footing, it is worth a brave searching for the why. It is worth taking care of yourself and seeing where some parts of your life might need to be confronted head-on and rebuilt—even wrangled down to the foundation. It is worth asking other people to take care of you too.

SOME CALM AND GENTLE PEOPLE IN MY LIFE

_____

_____

_____

_____

_____

_____

_____

_____

Broken Eggs

I KNOW I HAD DONE IT MANY TIMES, so I'm not sure why it caught my eye this particular time. But I remember looking down at the fried egg I was serving myself—and the ones I was sliding onto plates for Ryan and our kids—and realized I was in the habit of taking the broken or mangled one for myself.

I chose the egg that was a little overcooked or funny shaped or smaller than the others. It wasn't because anyone ever complained about a poorly fried egg; they were thankful to be fed and told me so. And I don't care enough about the shape or demeanor of a fried egg to mind if it's not perfect. I'm a lover of rough drafts and fraying fabric, so imperfection is fine by me. But I noticed that was what I always did with eggs: I took the lesser one. And I wondered if maybe that comes from this long-held agreement I had with myself to be "low maintenance."

I want to be easy to have around. Easy to like, easy to deal with, easy to lead, easy to hold on to. Easy feels peaceful, the kind of person others want in their life—the one they'll keep around and not abandon. The one who gets picked for the team, the friendship, the job, the open seat.

I have longed for "peace" at all costs, but unfortunately, I have believed peace means ease. I've believed peace means no one gets upset or inconvenienced or has their feathers ruffled. And I must have believed that if I was good enough, everyone would treat me with value and take care of me too.

This isn't always how it plays out, and that's a really hard thing to face. There will be people in your life, as there have been in mine, who will not take care of you. Some people are unsafe, unfit to be part of your close circle, unwise to include in your days.

I used to feel terrible about admitting this. I used to try so hard to make everyone work or fit. I have done for others what they should do for themselves. I have enabled. And while everyone has as much value as the next, I no longer believe that I have to be the solution for every person or anyone who raises their hand. If you've gotten stuck in that place, I hope you can walk your way out too. We are not meant to be saviors.

I believe now that peace is when we take care of one another in a way that honors everyone's worth—including our own.

I finally told Ryan about how hard it was for me to take the good eggs, and he could hardly believe it. He had no idea I felt that way. He said, "Take the best ones every time, Liz!" And although we both know that I don't really need to or want to—it's that moment when someone looks you in the eye and tells you how much you matter.

We all need shelters—even the ones making them.

WHAT DO YOU NEED?

WHAT HAVE YOU
STOPPED ASKING FOR?

WHAT HAVE YOU CALLED
IMPOSSIBLE?

WHAT DO YOU NEED TO
GIVE UP SO YOU HAVE
SPACE FOR THE
EXCHANGE?

YOU ARE WORTH . . .

You are worth safe people.

You are worth being honored.

You are worth being paid attention to.

You are worth being sacrificed for.

You are worth being sheltered.

You are worth a meal at the table.

You are worth the time it takes to heal.

You are worth the space it takes to heal.

You are worth sun shining full on your face.

You are worth the finest focus.

You are worth time off.

You are worth being held.

You are worth someone's greatest effort.

You are worth just as much as they are worth.

You are worth being served the most perfectly fried egg.

When You Lose Someone

JENNIE'S DAD WAS PULLING his fishing boat out to the ocean when his heart stopped. His was a heart that seemed to anchor half the world.

I want to put something here—Jennie's words about finding her way out of the dark—because all of us will have someone in our life whose absence collapses us too. And I imagine we will also be on the other end of the line when our beloved friend or sister or neighbor is collapsing, and we can be there to hold them, to grip their shoulders and kiss their foreheads, to get down in the tear-drenched grass next to them if that's where they're kneeling and kneel there too.

I was not ready, Liz. Losing my dad was sudden and too soon. I didn't know how to get through the next moment, let alone the rest of my life in his absence.

I sent you that desperate text—to you, to my safest people. I told you I didn't think I could breathe. And instead of running from the rawness of my grief, you women were like warriors on my behalf. You let me wail and weep and didn't try to make it seem any less than it was. You knew what it was, and you stayed with me there. You brought me food and wine and flowers but also a constant stream of texts pouring out your hearts so I knew you felt the pain too. You told me all the things you saw in me that were reflections of my father, told me he wasn't gone because I resembled him in so many ways. And for the first time since his loss, he felt close in a way I could hold on to.

I had to walk through the darkest night, but I didn't walk it alone. The tears you all shed on my behalf were a baptism and a balm. Before this, I didn't know what it felt like to face gutting loss. But in that free fall, I've been surrounded and held up by others. Now I know this: it's possible to create a space for someone's pain, no matter how deep they fall into it, if you are willing to wait for them in the dark and keep reaching out your hand until they finally come up for air.

We've all had our hazardous duties, our traumas, whether big or slight. We've likely faced some of these, but maybe not all, so the remnants still pop up at strange times or in strange ways. If they remain unfaced, they churn below the surface until we eventually (and hopefully) realize that the sense of chaos or numbness is something to unearth and lay out in the daylight.

Sometimes we're at a traffic light three years later when it resurfaces. Sometimes we're listening to someone else's story and our heart drops for a minute. Sometimes we're watching our kids play and an unforeseen sadness takes over and we think, *Where did that come from? Why am I sad?*

We have to do the work of bringing it together. Looking at reality. Seeing how it hurt. Figuring out, then, how best to heal and face the next hard thing with a deepened resilience. It's those internal reunions, the quiet homecomings.

Trauma and suffering don't take you out of the running in this haven-making world. Past mistakes or losses or hardships or hazardous duties do not disqualify you from being part of a gentle, abundant, and hospitable life.

The deepest grace and compassion almost always come from those who have suffered and fought too.

Giovanna's Milk *

I was sick in Italy once, and our landlord, Giovanna, brought me warmed milk with a dash of sugar and grappa. We sat at her old table outside, and I leaned over the drink as she told me about its cure-all abilities while Ryan winked about it simply getting you tipsy enough to fall asleep and forget you were sick. Whatever magic happened, I was content. So now I give the recipe to you, adapted by my friend Nicole since she's way more Italian than me and I couldn't quite remember what Giovanna told me to do.

01 Slowly warm the milk and sugar in a saucepan until the sugar dissolves.

02 Remove from heat, add grappa, and stir. If you have a milk frother, that works well.

03 Pour into a teacup, sip slowly, and get well.

04 Optional: Add a stick of cinnamon to the milk as it heats. Or grate fresh nutmeg over the top before serving.

1 cup whole milk

1 tablespoon cane sugar

¼ cup grappa (beautiful options: Nardini Grappa Bianca or Sarpa di Poli, or try Poli Acquavite)

1 cinnamon stick or fresh nutmeg (optional)

A note about grappa: If you can't find quality grappa (a drop rubbed on the back of your hand should smell like freshly crushed grapes, not musk or wet dog), white rum works in a pinch. But it's the grappa that sings here, and you'll want to appreciate its melody.

Another note about grappa: You don't have to use it. Warm, sweetened milk is extravagant too.

---

* Recipe contributed by Nicole Ziza Bauer.

Opening Early

I BELIEVE, NOW, in opening the doors before you think you're ready. It keeps you humble; it keeps space available for others; it's an acknowledgment that perfect readiness is impossible anyway.

Instead, you hand off sacrificial content. You share a rough draft. You throw a party even if you have only half the supplies. You are not too proud. You are not too tightfisted. You keep it all very breathable so others can step into that breathable space with you and contribute, add their own offerings, and know that they, too, can live from a place of gentle readiness.

At the new house, the door handle is broken.

The mood is mediocre.

A dead bird lies next to a glass window.

I've had a flop of a day because I want everything to be grand but it's just average.

I'm opening the door anyway, because I'm getting myself out of the way.

I'm going to go to sleep before the work is done anyway.

I'm going to stop and sit by the fire with Ryan anyway.

We're going camping as a family anyway.

We're going to add a dog to the mix anyway.

We're going to believe we made a good choice anyway.

We're going to hold it all lightly anyway.

A few workers outside just needed to use the bathroom—that was this new house's opening day.

It was a small crew of men who were late to finish the wood siding on our house. Our family was moved in. And the head of our building project quietly asked if I wouldn't mind if they came in to use the restroom. I needed to leave the house, so I unlocked the door and said, "Sure."

The smallest thing you can imagine. As easy as turning a latch and checking to see if there was soap, a clean towel, a doormat. I drove away from the house to pick up my kids from school and thought, *And that's that. It's open.* No fanfare, no invitations or announcements, no buzz or glory or beautiful moment to photograph. I wasn't even there.

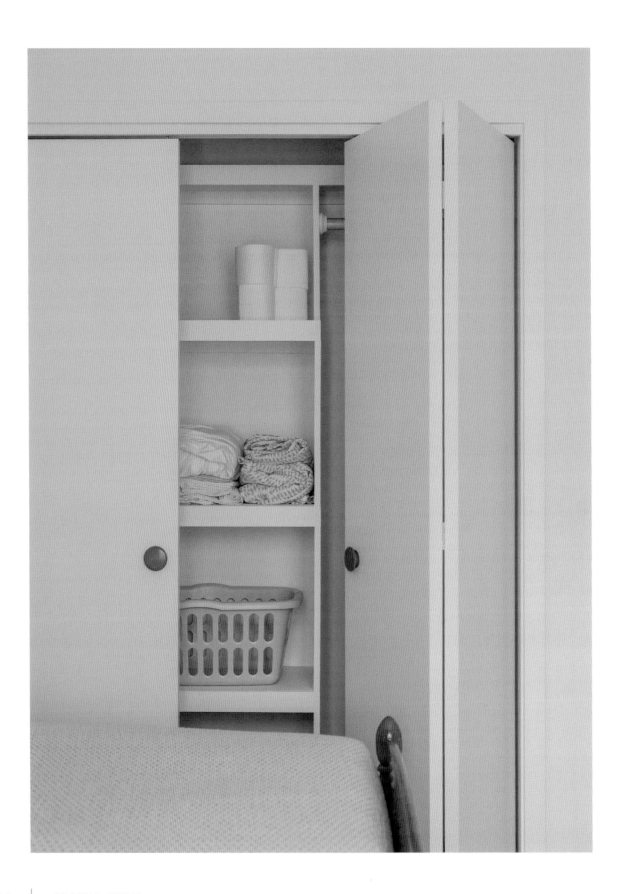

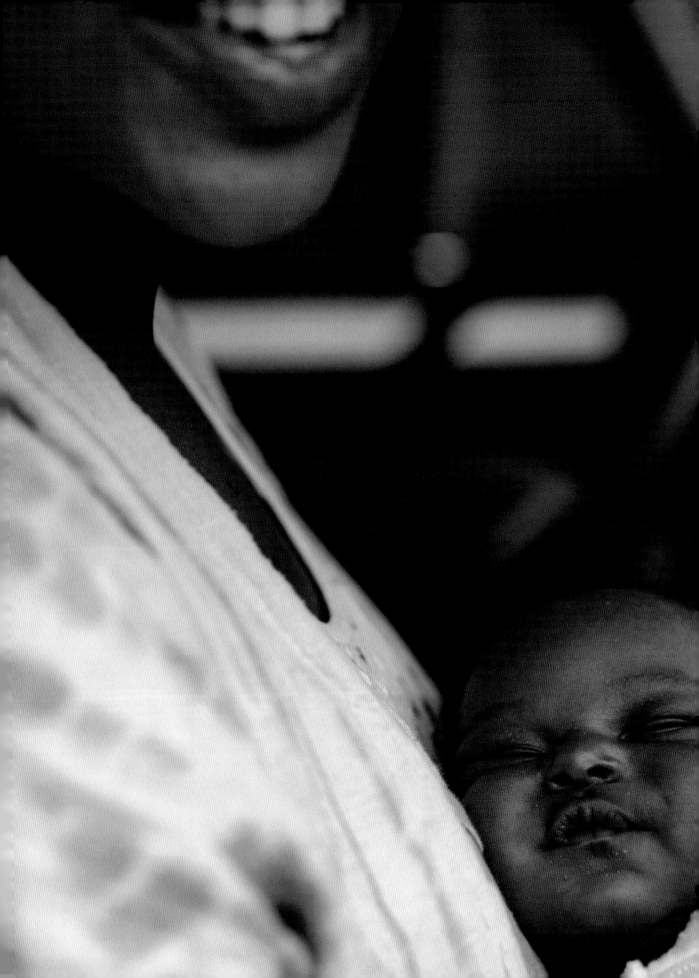

Sage-Orange Focaccia

with Honey, Black Pepper, and Rosemary Olive Oil

I love that this focaccia takes a little time. It's not a rush of a weeknight recipe. It's a thoughtful one—or a good one to make with overnight guests while you fill the fermenting and blooming and rising time with coffee and conversation.

FOR THE BREAD STARTER:

2 tablespoons warm water

4 tablespoons bread flour

2 teaspoons dry active yeast

01 In a small bowl, mix the warm water, flour, and yeast until cohesive.

02 Set aside to bloom for 30 minutes, uncovered, in a warm place.

FOR THE BREAD:

1¼ cup bread flour

1 cup warm water

bread starter

2⅛ teaspoons olive oil

1¼ teaspoons salt

Sage leaves (10–15)

1 orange

Flaky salt (for the topping)

01 In a large bowl—or the bowl of a stand mixer—mix the flour, water, and starter. The mixture will initially be shaggy in appearance. Continue mixing until combined and no dry flour is visible. Cover and allow to rest for 30 minutes at room temperature.

02 After the mixture has rested, add the olive oil and salt. Using your hands, massage the oil and salt into the dough. Once combined, knead by hand or use the dough hook attachment on a stand mixer, and mix until the dough becomes elastic and doesn't tear when stretched—roughly 8 to 10 minutes.

03 Cover and place in the fridge **for at least 12 hours**.

04 When you're ready to bake, oil a 10-inch pan. Then line the pan with parchment paper and generously oil the top of the paper. Pour the dough directly into the oiled, parchment-lined dish. Stretch and press down slightly. Allow to proof somewhere warm until doubled in size. This should take 1 to 1½ hours.

* Recipe contributed by Elise Smith.

05 While the bread proofs, wash and pat dry the sage leaves and orange. After removing the rind, slice the orange into circles and pat dry with a paper towel. Set both aside.

06 Preheat the oven to 445°F. After the dough has doubled in size, drizzle the top with a generous amount of olive oil and, with the tips of your fingers, dimple the bread.

07 Place the desired number of orange slices on top. Rub a bit of olive oil onto each of the sage leaves and adorn them across the surface. Finish with a healthy pinch of flaky salt. Bake for 25 minutes until golden brown. Allow to rest 10 minutes before cutting.

FOR THE INFUSED OIL:

2 large rosemary sprigs

¾ cup olive oil

⅓ cup honey

Fresh-cracked black pepper, to taste

01 Wash and pat dry the rosemary. Set aside. In a small saucepan over medium heat, add the olive oil. As it warms, lightly whack, roll, and press the sprigs of rosemary to release the oils in the leaves. Add the sprigs to the olive oil. Remove from heat just as the oil first pops (that's the water in the rosemary evaporating).

02 Set aside to cool, leaving the rosemary to steep. When the oil is cool, whisk together the honey, black pepper, and rosemary oil in a small serving bowl. Serve with the hot focaccia (or store in an airtight container in the fridge). Enjoy!

Daydreaming

I HOLD THE PHONE TO MY EAR as I pick up shells from the beach and shake off the sand, turn them around, see if anything is still alive inside. Anna is far away from where I am, telling me wistful things over the line, trying new ideas out loud from her state to mine. Her voice matches the waves that way, and I think about how people can do this for each other. We can let each other float things out in the air and see how they do.

We talk about white houses, seminary, soft T-shirts. We talk about things that make us tear up and wonder why they do. We talk about words we want to put on paper—and words we don't anymore. Before we hang up, she says, "Liz, when you daydream out loud with someone . . . when someone gives you the space to daydream . . . *that's* hospitality, isn't it?"

And I tell her that's the truth.

PEOPLE I CAN DAYDREAM WITH

_____

_____

_____

_____

_____

_____

_____

_____

_____

_____

HOW TO:

Make Friends and Dinner

*Beam on the people who come to your door. Find people who beam
   back on you.*
Invite them to dinner. Make it a beautiful potluck.
*Listen long and well at the table, without turning their stories quickly
   back to your own.*
Be generous and honest with your own stories and responses.
Ask each other, "What makes you feel alive right now?"
Ask each other, "What's weighing you down?"
*Remember, later, what others shared. Remind them what you care
   about too.*
*Laugh hard and say ridiculous or audacious things. It brings healing
   through the side doors.*
*Don't run from sadness in the midst of lightheartedness. It can all live
   together.*
If someone needs a place to stay, give them a key.
Hand out coffee and bread in the morning.

I hadn't planned long for it, but suddenly it seemed the thing to do:
bring a few friends over, eat a warm meal, circle around a table. A few
of the women came with overnight bags; one came with a baby; one
came with an empty nest. One asked me ahead of time if it was going
to be okay not knowing anyone else, and I said, "Yes, it's a good thing
to do—they are kind women."

Late that night, one of my kind friends sat on the roof by herself after everyone had left or fallen asleep. She needed space to think and a pen to hold, both of which I had to give. She's a lover of messages, and she found one attached to her tea. She left this on my table in the morning:

"May your head and your heart
speak with one voice."

I let those words—the message on my tea bag,
sink under the surface, as I wait for water

to boil. It's midnight and I'm perched on a
slick rooftop, inhaling the hushed-night sky,

slow-pulling up the glory spent with women
moments ago, at a dinner table down below.

Open chests, captured by a lens. A whole grove of women,
like trees, surrounded me: grounded, resilient, wise.

We passed platters of dreams, and bread. We peeled it back:
potatoes, and red wine—considering prayer, unbridled horses.

A baby swelled with delight, at the breast
of a girl I watched bloom into a sure-footed mother.

Not a phone in sight; bright faces by
candlelight whispering love, loss: the sacred both/and.

Tea-empty, belly-full, I fold myself into pockets
of home, I know: the divine message spoken.

My head and my heart aligned—
one honest, ardent voice.

KRISTIN ROARK

Brides

NEXT WEEK WE'RE TAKING Woman Camp on the road—taking it into a women's prison. We have sent in our forms to get security clearance; we know we're not allowed to wear open-toed shoes or bring glass or metal. Instead of setting up in a field, we'll set up in a gym. Instead of making campfires, we'll use food that's already been prepared. No wandering through the woods. No swinging from trees or slinging firewood into a pickup truck. But we will bring in spools of twine, cloth banners, buckets of flowers, a feast.

One hundred women will be there to receive it.

LaTasha comes over to my house so we can run over the things we'll say from whatever kind of stage we can set up. We hit a few walls as we sort our way through the words we'll share—we know there are certain things that are not helpful to say to women who no longer have physical freedom. But there is something we have in common, no matter where we sleep at night or what we've done or how many traumas we've caused or survived: we each hold immense value. So this is what we will say to one another, and what we will say to the hundred women:

WE ALL HAVE
A PLACE AT
THE TABLE.

Then we will set up feast tables in their gym— because years ago, when we dreamed up what a Woman Camp experience could be, Jennie believed that everyone needs to know she has a place prepared for her—a lavish place. Everyone needs to know she is chosen. And I realize the powerful truth of this too, now that we've had thousands of place cards handwritten in gold, then set at the places for all the women who come to take part. Place cards that women keep next to their beds, taped to their mirrors. Their names, their value.

I don't know what parts of this next story to tell— what it was like to be there in the prison, to be welcomed and received there, to be both wrecked and awestruck there. It's too soon to see it in hindsight, and this may take years. But one thing happened that I want to tell now.

The gym at the prison sits low, sunken below the rest of the building. So to get to it, you have to walk down a wide staircase.

Our one hundred guests had to leave the Woman Camp event right in the middle of it for an hour, escorted outside by security guards, to make sure everyone was accounted for. While the women were away, we had that hour to fly around the gym shaking out black linen tablecloths, turning on battery-operated candlesticks, piling high the serving platters with roasted chickens, citrusy greens, baguettes, honey butter. Every woman's place setting was golden, white, shining. Every place card was written and ready: her first name, her last name. We turned on music and wiped the sweat off our faces just in time for the doors to open again.

And then one of our leaders ran to the foot of the staircase and started cheering wildly when the first guest stood at the top of the stairs, paused, and then began to wind her way down. She was beaming. And after a minute, the rest of us joined the cheering brigade, forming an arch above their heads, our hands reaching as close to them as we were allowed.

Some women covered their faces with their hands, laughing, blushing. Some women started dancing. Some were quiet. And one woman came through twice, which thrilled everyone to no end. I heard one woman say to another woman, "Like we're brides."

Holy Bins

WE PILE INTO THE VAN: Ryan, the kids, me. The trunk is full of sleeping bags, gallons of water, boots. We're leaving for Family Camp to join hundreds of other families. For every adult reason, it's not a good or responsible time for us to leave. We have too much work in front of us and not much left in the tank.

At our house, they're building a stone wall and will be making decisions without us. I should be finishing my writing deadlines behind lock and key. Ryan is craving a quiet weekend after long weeks of fixing broken things all around the city. But we promised our friends we'd be at camp; we promised the kids and told them it's important. And this is how it always seems to feel before you leave: not the right time—until you get there.

We pitch a tent, prop open the top of the camper van, roll out blankets. Our friends are already there, and they've backed up their pickup trucks and vans to create a little camp town. One dad strings up a hammock so the kids can dive in, eat candy. The adults start conversations and reunite. We have seventeen kids between us, and they throw footballs and drag around sticks and open all the coolers to see what's in store for the night.

The scene from that California beach when I sat alone with my dinner in a plastic bag—it's unfolding again. But this time I'm not watching it unfold; I'm inside of it. It's not an idyllic beach, but it's Ohio and it's home and it's family.

It was the second night of camp when our family went into the prayer tent. We sat on the hay bales and huddled in close. The people who were running the tent had put three clear plastic bins at every hay bale area, and your family was supposed to choose one, follow the prompts inside.

When I sat down with our youngest on my lap and looked over at the bins next to us, I just stared in disbelief at what was inside. It was a little old book with rabbits on the front. A mother and her bunny. One who wanted to run away. One who said she'd follow no matter what.

I looked around the prayer tent and saw the same book inside every third bin. It was a tent full of runaway bunnies. A tent full of homecoming.

Let There Be Havens

LET THERE BE HAVENS.

On hay bales.

In the lamplight of homes.

On sidewalks and grocery stores
and countries not our own.

In vans, garages, fields.

In passing moments.

In long conversations.

In the sharing of lives.

Let there be people who love one another, watch
out for one another, shelter one another. Let there
be open doors and beaming faces, gentle conversations and steady landings, calmly held boundaries,
and our worth upheld.

Let there be you.

Acknowledgments

To Wendell, for that Sunday in your kitchen and always writing back.

To Joy, who waves her wand from Paris and is the best agent in the whole world.

To Tyndale, who fits like a glove.

To Jillian and Stephanie, who said it matters and let me run.

To Jennie, for saying write it, release it, believe it.

To Charis, for cheering wildly and keeping our hopes up.

To Bukovec, for your gorgeous visions and popping up like a genie every time.

To DVal, who designs like a dream and brings the sunshine.

To Cindy and Kerri, for propping me up before this even started.

To J&K, Ken, Elam, Hartigan, Drawing Department, Ron and Suz; for getting this house off the ground with us.

To Lori, for keeping me healthy so I could write.

To Debbie, for saying goodwill is a message the world needs to hear.

To Kaila, who challenged me to go further—right out of the gates.

To Gary, who opened new doors at the perfect time.

To BT and Crossroads Church, for your aggressive spirit and pushing outside the walls.

To my parents, for bringing me here and holding on so well.

To my sisters, my Little Women.

To my three children: you are dreams; you are stars.

To Ryan. You are the one.